PENGUIN BOOKS
TALES OF THE OPEN ROAD

Ruskin Bond was born in Kasauli in 1934, and grew up in Jamnagar, Dehradun, New Delhi and Simla. As a young man, he spent four years in the Channel Islands and London. He returned to India in 1955, and has never left the country since. His first novel, *The Room on the Roof*, received the John Llewellyn Rhys Prize, awarded to a Commonwealth writer under thirty, for 'a work of outstanding literary merit'. He has, since, published over thirty-five books, including the novellas *A Flight of Pigeons* and *Delhi Is Not Far*, and several collections of short stories. He received a Sahitya Akademi Award in 1993, and the Padma Shri in 1999.

He lives in Landour, Mussoorie, with his extended family.

ALSO BY RUSKIN BOND

Fiction
The Room on the Roof & Vagrants in the Valley
The Night Train at Deoli and Other Stories
Time Stops at Shamli and Other Stories
Our Trees Still Grow in Dehra
Strangers in the Night: Two Novellas
A Season of Ghosts
When Darkness Falls and Other Stories
A Flight of Pigeons
Delhi Is Not Far
A Face in the Dark and Other Hauntings

Non-fiction
Rain in the Mountains
Scenes from a Writer's Life
The Lamp Is Lit
The Little Book of Comfort
Landour Days
Book of Nature

Anthologies
Collected Fiction (1955–1996)
The Best of Ruskin Bond
Friends in Small Places
Indian Ghost Stories (ed.)
Indian Railway Stories (ed.)
Classic Indian Love Stories and Lyrics (ed.)

Tales of the Open Road

Ruskin Bond

PENGUIN BOOKS

An imprint of Penguin Random House

PENGUIN BOOKS

USA | Canada | UK | Ireland | Australia
New Zealand | India | South Africa | China | Singapore

Penguin Books is part of the Penguin Random House group of companies
whose addresses can be found at global.penguinrandomhouse.com

Published by Penguin Random House India Pvt. Ltd
4th Floor, Capital Tower 1, MG Road,
Gurugram 122 002, Haryana, India

First published by Penguin Books India 2006

Copyright © Ruskin Bond 2006

13 12 11 10 9 8

ISBN 9780144000722

Typeset in *PalmSprings* by SÜRYA, New Delhi

Printed at Manipal Technologies Limited, India

All photographs, except those on pages 74 and 117, by Ruskin Bond.

www.penguin.co.in

MIX
Paper | Supporting
responsible forestry
FSC® C043100

CONTENTS

The Open Road

Out of the city and over the hill,
Into the spaces where Time stands still,
Under the tall trees, touching old wood,
Taking the way where warriors once stood;
Crossing the little bridge, losing my way,
Finding a friendly place where I could stay.
Those were the days, friend, when we were strong
And strode down the road to an old marching song,
When the dew on the grass was fresh every morn,
And we woke to the call of the ring-dove at dawn.
The years have gone by, and sometimes I falter,
But still I set out for a stroll or a saunter,
For the wind is as fresh as it was in our youth,
And the peach and the pear still the sweetest of fruit.
So cast away care and come roaming with me,
And know what it is to be perfectly free.

—Ruskin Bond

INTRODUCTION

So far as I know, the only member of my family who did a lot of walking was my grandfather, Henry William Bond, and he did so because he was a foot-soldier, and did not have much choice in the matter.

Nevertheless, I might have inherited his ability to cover long distances, at a steady, unhurried pace, covering some fifteen miles a day—as he must have done before setting up camp off the Grand Trunk Road or, later, in one of the many cantonments that came up in the nineteenth century.

My grandfather always knew what place he needed to reach, and would usually have taken the shortest route to get there. But I have come to believe that the best kind of walk, or journey, is the one in which you have no particular destination when you set out.

This is particularly useful in a city or town that you are new to. The ideal way to get to know it is to walk its streets, and this is what I did during my sojourns in London, Delhi, Dehra Dun, Saharanpur and elsewhere.

When I was twenty, and living in London, I would spend my weekends walking the East End, the Nile End Road, Dockland—Dicken's London—or the many parks that dotted that 'green city'—Hampstead Heath, Primrose Hill, Hyde Park, Kensington Gardens, which of course I associated with Peter Pan, the first literary figure of my childhood reading. I lived in the Hampstead area, and worked in an office on the Tottenham Court Road, and sometimes I would walk to work (much nicer than the tube train), over Primrose Hill and down to Baker Street. It took me a little over an hour, if I remember correctly. Grandfather would have been proud of me.

Back in Dehra Dun in 1955, I walked all over the place. My landlady, who was also my stepfather's first wife, called me the 'road inspector'. But it was a small town then, and a half-hour walk would take me across the dry river-bed and into the tea gardens or sal forest. I was a lonely walker. Not many people cared to walk all day, then or now. I seem to have had much more time on my hands when I was a young man. How come I'm having to work harder at age seventy? Now, if I want a walk, I have to get up at five a.m., so that I'm back at my desk at seven. And then breakfast beckons . . . There's nothing like a good breakfast after an early morning walk. A scrambled egg, some marmalade on toast, and just a little bacon please.

When I was based in Delhi for some years in the fifties and sixties, I continued with my habit of long walks. Winter evenings I would occasionally walk from Connaught Place to Patel Nagar or even all the way to Rajouri Garden (through the Pusa Institute grounds);

this took a couple of hours or more. On the way I would pass street vendors selling boiled eggs. I ate a lot of eggs. We hadn't heard about cholesterol in those days.

Of course the best walks are to be enjoyed in the hills, preferably in the company of a quiet friend. Sometimes I would escape from Delhi and trek to the Pindari Glacier in Kumaon, or the hills beyond Landsdowne, or Deoban above Chakrata. I wasn't interested in climbing mountains—I preferred going around them: you saw more that way. At every bend of the road in the mountains there is a fresh vista, a different landscape, interesting people, new birds, trees, flowers.

Some of these excursions could be quite comical. On one occasion, many years ago, a Bengali friend and I decided to walk from Mussoorie to Chamba (near Tehri), some thirty miles distant. This was before the road became motorable.

I knew we wouldn't find anything to eat along the way, so I slipped two tins of sardines into my haversack and we set off on our day-long walk. By noon we were both quite hungry, so we sat down in the shade of a whispering pine, and quenched our thirst from our water bottles. Then, with a flourish, I produced the sardine tins.

To my horror I discovered I'd left the tin-opener behind. We did our best to open the tins with stones and even a horseshoe nail, but to no avail.

'Why couldn't you remind me to bring a tin-opener along?' I snapped at my companion. 'You're a Bengali, you're supposed to like fish.'

'Only fresh-water Hilsa,' he replied disdainfully. 'We don't go in for tinned stuff.'

In my frustration I flung both tins into a deep ravine, and for all I know they are still there, unless aliens from outer space have succeeded in opening them.

At Chamba we found a tea shop that sold some ancient, rock-hard buns, probably left behind by the roving Pandavas. We softened them up by soaking them in mugs of hot tea, and so satisfied our hunger to some extent.

Two days later, on our return to Dehra, the first thing I saw was the tin-opener on my desk.

These are journeys I still remember for the grace and beauty of the landscape, the clean, sharp air and clear waters. But there were others, to places far less inspiring, that I will never forget. Human beings and the worlds they make for themselves are as fascinating as the wonders of Nature. You will find something to surprise or amuse you even in the dullest of places, as I did in several small towns around Delhi and Dehra.

Shahjahanpur, Chhutmulpur, Shamli, Kotdwar . . . There was little to distinguish many of them. All their

bazaars were chaotic, most of the roads narrow and dusty and the majority of their inhabitatnts poor and weary. But some scene on a deserted road, a chance encounter, a memorable meal or a neglected monument would give each one a special character.

* * *

It is close to three decades now since I undertook a long journey into the hills or on the highway with no fixed destination in mind. I travel only when I have to, and when I do, I notice how much things have changed.

That old mule-track to Tehri is now a busy thoroughfare and you won't go hungry along the way. There's fast food everywhere.

Some places change quite dramatically over the years. Forty years ago, when I first visited Bangalore, I walked out to the Sampingi Tank, where boys swam around a little island and washed down their buffaloes. On a recent visit I tried to find the Tank, struggling down roads filled with snarling traffic, but it appeared to have vanished. High-rise buildings had come up where once old bungalows and gardens characterized the city.

Delhi, too, has spread out in all directions and the wilderness that was Tughlaqabad or Suraj Kund is now part of Greater Delhi.

But some places have resisted change. I walked down Atul Grove Road in the heart of New Delhi, and was pleasantly surprised to find that it looked no different from the way it had been back in 1943, when I had stayed there with my father. One of those quiet corners which had escaped the frenzy of the growing city.

The world keeps changing, but there is always something, somewhere, that remains the same.

November 2005

The Open Road

THE OPEN ROAD

ON THE HIGHWAY

For forty years I have been content living a life of modest excitements in Mussoorie. The world drives up here in season, for holidays and honeymoons, so I rarely feel the need to go down to the busy plains. But once or twice a year, in self-indulgent mood, or when my publishers prevail upon me, I give myself a 'treat', if you can call it that: a seven-hour drive to Delhi in a sturdy Ambassador taxi. Winter is the best time for such a visit. The hot winds of summer are best avoided, for once you have descended from the hills, the road becomes dusty, and in places something of an obstacle race.

I have known this highway over the years and I have seen it change imperceptibly. There wasn't much traffic on it in the 1940s, apart from the familiar bullock carts stacked high with sugarcane. The carts are still used, although the wooden wheels have given way to heavy tyres, and the bullocks to buffaloes. However, much of the sugarcane is now carried in trucks, and these 'kings of the road' have made it difficult for others to drive smoothly by day or safely by night. But I am told the trucks and the sugarcane keep the economy of the region going, so we shouldn't grumble too much.

I am told the same about all the cars and tourist buses that I complain about: what would happen to Uttaranchal's economy if they stopped coming! I quieten down then, but I wonder at the great speed at which they move. People come seeking Nature and new experiences but have no interest in the world outside.

To me, the outside world is the reward of a highway journey. I like looking at the countryside, the passing scene, the people along the road (so it is just as well that I cannot drive). And even in the twenty-first century, when television channels claim to show us everything there is to see, it can be a revelation. Recently, on a trip to Delhi, we had to leave the main highway because of a disturbance near Meerut. Instead we had to drive through about a dozen villages in the sugarcane belt that dominates this area. It was a wonderful contrast, leaving the main road with its cafes, petrol pumps, factories and management institutes and entering the rural hinterland where very little had changed in a hundred years. Women with their faces veiled worked in the fields, old men smoked hookahs in their courtyards, and a few children were playing guli-danda instead of cricket! It brought home to me the reality of India—urban life and rural life are still poles apart.

As I do not drive myself, I am the ideal person to have in the front seat; I repose complete confidence in the man behind the wheel. Sitting up front, I also see more of the road and the passing scene. Sardar Manmohan Singh shares this interest, but he has a far sharper eye. Manmohan is one of Mussoorie's better taxi drivers. He is also a keen wildlife enthusiast. It always amazes me how he is able to drive through the Siwaliks, on a winding hill road, and still be able to keep his eye open for denizens of the surrounding forest.

'See that cheetal!' he will exclaim, or 'What a fine sambhar!' or 'Just look at that elephant!'

All this at high speed. And before I've had time to get more than a fleeting glimpse of one of these creatures, we are well past them.

Manmohan swears that he has seen a tiger crossing the road near the Mohand Pass, and as he is a person of some integrity, I have to believe him. I think the tiger appears especially for Manmohan.

Another wildlife enthusiast is my bank manager and old friend Vishal Ohri, with whom I have been on some memorable drives. Unlike our car drivers, he is in no hurry to reach our destination and will stop every now and then, in order to examine the footprints of an elephant or a leopard. He also takes great pleasure in pointing out large dollops of fresh elephant dung, proof that wild elephants are in the vicinity. The prospect of being charged by an angry elephant has never worried him, and he holds forth at great length on the benefits of elephant dung—how it can be used to reinforce mud walls, for instance—till I urge him to get a move on before nightfall.

On one occasion, Vishal decided to give me a treat by taking a short cut from Hardwar through the Rajaji Sanctuary and out at the Mohand Pass. Vishal enjoys his driving, especially in rough conditions; unfortunately, his ancient Fiat was in poor condition, and halfway through the sanctuary, while we were crossing a boulder-strewn *rao* (a semi-dry riverbed) the door on my side fell off and I very nearly went with it. For the rest of the journey, I had an uninterrupted view of the wildlife in the sanctuary—two peahens, a startled porcupine, and a herd of tame buffaloes.

* * *

Driving by night is not always so risible. Most accidents on the main highway road occur in the early hours when drivers fall asleep at the wheel: their vehicles overturn, or run into trees and ditches, or collide with other vehicles. Before dawn breaks, the road has taken its toll of several lives.

It was late Christmas Eve in the 1970s, when my thirty-year-old half-brother Harold set out from Dehra in his father's car, to try and get to Delhi in time for a party at the Anglo-Indian Club. Although he was a good driver, having taken part in car rallies and other tests of speed and endurance, he had become a heavy drinker and he was in no condition to undertake a long and arduous drive late at night. He was alone, and as he was killed instantly (or so we were told), we never knew all the circumstances of his death. Apparently his car had been caught and crushed between two trucks, which had speedily disappeared into the night.

Harold was always a bit of a tearaway. He was attractive to women, but they had a hard time looking after him. And he wrecked their lives in addition to his own. There were lessons about life and highways that he never learnt.

But perhaps there aren't any lessons to be learnt. A few months after Harold, my second half-brother was killed in a motorcycle accident. He was the careful one, who seldom took risks. He was sober that night, as on all others, and mindful of rules, but someone else on the road was not.

THE GRAND TRUNK ROAD

There is a fantasy journey that I have always wanted to make, but one that I know I never will: the long, long journey along the Grand Trunk Road from Calcutta to Peshawar.

For the Grand Trunk Road is a river. It may not be as sacred as the Ganga, which it greets at Kanpur and Varanasi, but it is just as permanent. It's a river of life, an unending stream of humanity intent on reaching their destination and getting there most of the time.

A long day's journey into night, that's how I would describe the saga of the truck driver, that knight errant, or rather errant knight, of India's Via Appia. Undervalued, underpaid and often disparaged, he drives all day and sometimes all night, carrying the country's goods and produce for hundreds of miles on the GT Road, across state borders, through lawless tracts, at all seasons and in all weathers. We blame him for hogging the middle of the road, but he is usually overloaded and if he veers too much to the left or right he is quite likely to topple over, burying himself and crew under bricks or gas cylinders, sugarcane or TV sets. More than the railwayman, the truck driver is modern India's lifeline, and yet his life is held cheap. He drinks, he swears, occasionally he picks up HIV, and frequently he is killed or badly injured. But we cannot do without him.

In the old, old days, when Muhammad Tughlaq, Sultan of Delhi, streamlined the country's roads, bullock carts and camel caravans were the chief transporters. In 1333, when the Moroccan traveller Ibn Battuta visited India, he was deeply impressed by the Sultan's road network. Sher Shah Suri, who ruled from 1540 till 1545, made further improvements, especially to the GT Road. He built caravanserais and inns for travellers, and planted fine trees along the GT Road and other important highways. Horsemen, carts and palanquin bearers jostled for pride of position, much as our motorists do today. Traffic was slow-moving, and the best way to get ahead was to mount a horse and canter from stage to stage, that is, between twelve and fifteen miles a day.

Invading armies had, of course, made use of the Road long before the British gained control of northern India. On this same stretch of the highway, the Persian invader Nadir Shah defeated the Mughal Emperor in 1739. In a battle lasting two hours, over 20,000 of the Emperor's soldiers were killed. The next day Nadir Shah marched to Delhi, to sack the city and massacre its inhabitants. The treasure harvest of Delhi was fair game for acquisitive kings and warlords.

When the British consolidated their power in India, they found the Road, stretching as it did from Calcutta to Peshawar, a great line of communication. Kipling's 'regiment a-marchin' down the GT Road' was a common enough sight throughout the nineteenth century. During the 1857 uprising, after the British were ousted from Delhi, their army assembled at Ambala and came marching down the GT Road to lay siege to the city of Delhi. A few years later a junior officer, recalling the march, wrote:

> The stars were bright in the dark deep sky and the fireflies flashed from bush to bush . . . Along the road came the heavy roll of the guns, mixed with the jangling of bits and the clanking of the scabbards of the cavalry. The infantry marched behind with a deep, dull tread. Camels and bullock carts, with innumerable camp servants, toiled away for miles in the rear, while gigantic

elephants, pulling the heavy guns, came lumbering down the road.

Some thirty years after the 1857 uprising came the Afghan Wars, and the GT Road became an all-important route for the British army proceeding towards Peshawar and the Khyber Pass. Those were the days of military manoeuvres all over north India, and my grandfather, a foot-soldier in the mould of Kipling's 'soldiers three', found himself 'route marching', that is, foot-slogging all over northern and central India. Wives and children followed the regiment wherever it was sent, and military camps and cantonments sprang up everywhere. Children were often born in the course of these marches and troop movements: my father at Shahjahanpur (not far from the Road), his brothers and sisters at places as far apart as Barrackpore, Campbellpur and Dera Ismail Khan!

The tedium of the march was broken only by the sight of fields of golden corn stretching towards the horizon, with mango groves rising like islands from the flat plain; but for the most part it was monotonous tramping, exemplified in this marching song of Kipling's:

Oh, there's them Indian temples to admire when
    you see,
There's the peacock round the corner

An' the monkey up the tree.
With our best foot first
And the Road a-sliding past,
An' every bloomin' camping-ground
Exactly like the last.

Kipling immortalized the Road in *Kim* and *Barrack-Room Ballads* (he had a strong empathy with the common soldier), and but for him, few outside of India would have heard of the Grand Trunk Road. But Kipling would not recognize the Road today. Cars, buses, tractors, trucks, all thunder down the highway, and even the bullock carts are equipped with heavy tyres. It's a very democratic mix. Nowhere else in the world are you likely to find such a variety of traffic, or so many impediments to vehicular progress—cows, cart-horses, buffaloes, cyclists, stray hens, stray villagers, stray policemen.

'Proceed at Your Own Risk.' You could call this the motto of the Road, a motto vividly illustrated by overturned lorries lying in ditches, buses upended against trees or dangling over culverts, fancy cars crushed into concertina shapes, squashed cats and dogs, mangled drivers and passengers. These are common sights, along with the endless panorama of field, factory, village or township.

For the towns and cities grow bigger by the day. They spread octopus-like over the rural landscape, and the traffic spills out in an endless, honking procession of humankind on wheels. 'OK Tata', proclaims the truck in front of you, and it would be wise to keep your distance. What's your choice of vehicle for making progress on the Road? Motorcycle, taxi, limousine, or buffalo cart? Mine's a steamroller. No one pushes it around.

* * *

I have never travelled the entire length of the Road, but I have driven along stretches of it. The most memorable one was with Gurbachan Singh.

As his taxi weaved its way in and out of the Amritsar traffic, and headed for Delhi, Gurbachan Singh took his hand off the horn and gave me a brief triumphant look.

'What do you think of my horn?' he asked.

'Oh, it's a fine horn,' I said, wringing out my ears. 'It couldn't be louder.'

'You can hear it half a mile ahead,' said Gurbachan proudly, as he blasted off at two young men who were sharing a bicycle. They moved out of the way with alacrity.

'It makes a lot of noise in the car, too,' I said, and added hastily, 'not that I object, you know . . .'

'Doesn't your horn have more than one tone of voice?' asked a fellow traveller with a trace of irritation.

'Two!' claimed Gurbachan. 'Male and female. Just see!' And he produced a high note and then a low note on the horn, both equally ear-shattering. Ahead of us, a tonga ran off the road and on to the cart track.

'This is one terrific horn,' said Gurbachan. 'I have had it made especially for this taxi. No foreign horns for me. They are not loud enough. Indian horns are best.'

'Indian noise is best,' said the fellow traveller.

In an interval of comparative quiet, I found myself reflecting on the nature of sound—the unpleasantness of some sounds, and the sweetness of others, and why certain sounds (like motor horns) can be sweet to some and hideous to others. The sweetest sound of all, I decided, was silence. There are many kinds of silence—the silence of an empty room, the silence of the mountains, the silence of prayer, or the enforced silence of loneliness—but the best kind of silence, I concluded, was the silence that comes after the cessation of noise.

'It was made in the Jama Masjid area,' continued Gurbachan, interrupting my thoughts. 'Seventy-five rupees only. Made by hand, to my own specification. There's only one drawback: it must not get wet!'

As his hand settled down on the horn again, I

thought of praying for rain, but the sky being clear and blue, I decided that a prayer would be an unreasonable demand on the Creator.

'Ah, but you don't know what it is to have a horn like this one. Try it, sir. Why don't you try it for yourself?'

'Oh, that's all right,' I assured him. 'You have proved its excellence already.'

'No, you must try it. I insist that you try it!' He was like a big boy, suddenly generous, determined on sharing a new toy with a younger brother.

He grabbed my hand and placed it on the horn, and, as I felt it give a little, a thrill of pleasure rushed up my arm. I pressed hard, and a stream of music flowed in and out of the car. Now I could understand the happiness and the supreme self-confidence of Gurbachan and all drivers like him; for, with a horn like his, one felt the power and glory that belongs to the kings of the Road.

For the rest of the journey Gurbachan drove and I blew the horn.

The fellow passenger, no doubt realizing that he was locked into a taxi with two lunatics, was too terrified to say a word.

RUNNING AWAY

Once, during my schooldays, my friend Daljit and I decided to run away. The main reason for running away was not to get back to the bazaars of Dehra, which we both missed, but to reach my uncle's ship in Jamnagar, Gujarat.

Uncle Jim was one of my father's cousins. He used to write to me off and on throughout the years. His letters came in envelopes that bore colourful stamps of different countries. They came from Valparaiso, San Diego, San Francisco, Buenos Aires, Dar-es-Salaam, Mombasa, Freetown, Singapore, Bombay, Marseilles, London . . . these were some of the places where Uncle Jim's ship called. He was seldom on the same route, and seemed to move leisurely across the oceans of the earth, calling at ports which had only the most romantic associations for me, for I had already read Stevenson, Captain Marryat, some Conrad and W.W. Jacobs.

In his letters, Uncle Jim often spoke of my joining him at sea—'When you are a little older, Ruskin.'

But I felt I was old enough then. I was sick of school and sick of my guardian. But that was not all. I was in love with the world. I wanted to see the world, every corner of it, the places I had read about in books—the junks and sampans of Hong Kong, the palm-fringed lagoons of the Indies, the streets of London, the beautiful ebony-skinned people of Africa, the bright birds and exotic plants of the Amazon . . .

When Uncle Jim's last letter had arrived, telling me that his ship would call at Jamnagar towards the end of the month, I felt a deep thrill of anticipation. Here was my chance at last! True, Uncle Jim had said nothing about my joining him, but he was not to know that I was seriously considering it.

It was not simply a question of walking out of school and taking a quick ride down to the docks. Jamnagar, on the west coast, was at least eight hundred miles from my school. I doubt if I would have made the attempt if Daljit had not agreed to come too. It isn't much fun running away on your own. It is even worse if you have a companion who is full of enthusiasm at the beginning and who backs out at the last moment. This leaves one feeling defeated and crushed. Daljit was not that kind of companion. He meant the things he said. About a month earlier, when I had told him of my uncle's ship and my wish to get to it, he had said, without a moment's hesitation: 'I'm coming too!' Daljit lived impulsively. Sometimes he made mistakes. But he never went halfway and stopped. Someone had to stop him; otherwise he did whatever it was he set out to do.

Running away from school! It is not to be recommended to everyone. Parents and teachers would disapprove. Or would they, deep down in their hearts? Everyone has wanted to run away, at some time in his life: if not from a bad school or an unhappy home, then from something equally unpleasant. Running away seems to be in the best of traditions. Huck Finn did it. So did Master Copperfield and Oliver Twist. So did Kim. Various enterprising young men have run away to sea. Most great men have run away from school at some stage in their lives; and if they haven't, then perhaps it is something they should have done.

Anyway, Daljit and I ran away from school, and we did it quite successfully too, up to a point. But then, all this happened in India, which, though it forms only two per cent of the world's land mass, has 15 per cent of its population, and so it is an easy place to hide in, or be lost in, or disappear in, and never be seen or heard of again!

Not that we intended to disappear. We were headed for a particular place, and as soon as I took my first step into the unknown, that first step on the slippery pine needles below the school, I knew quite definitely that I wasn't running away from anything, but that I was running *towards* something. Call it a dream, if you like. I was running towards a dream.

A narrow path ran downhill from the school to the road to Dehra, and we followed it until it levelled out, running parallel with the small stream that rumbled down the mountainside. We followed the stream for a mile, walking swiftly and silently, until we met the bridle-path which was little more than a mule-track going steeply down the last hills to the valley.

The going was easy. We knew the road well. And by the time we reached the last foothills it was beginning to rain, not heavily, but as a light, thin drizzle.

We took shelter in a small dhaba on the outskirts of a village. The dhabawallah was sleeping, and his dog, a mangy pariah with only one ear, sniffed at us in a friendly way instead of chasing us off the premises. We sat down on an old bench and watched the sun rising over the distant mountains.

This is something I have always remembered. Not because it was a more beautiful sunrise than on any other day, but because the special importance of that morning made me look at everything in a new way, hence the details still stand out in my memory.

As the sky grew lighter, the pines and deodars stood out clearly, and the birds came to life. A black-bird started it all with a low, mellow call, and then the thrushes began chattering in the bushes. A barbet shrieked monotonously at the top of a spruce tree, and, as the sky grew lighter still, a flock of bright green parrots flew low over the trees.

The drizzle continued and there was a bright crimson glow in the east. And then, quite suddenly, the sun shot through a gap in the clouds, and the lush green monsoon grass sprang into relief. Both Daljit and I were wonderstruck. Never before had we been up so early. Hundreds of spiderwebs, which were spun in trees and bushes and on the grass, where they would not normally have been noticed, were now clearly visible, spangled with gold and silver raindrops. The strong silk threads of the webs held the light rain and the sun, making each drop of water look like a tiny jewel.

A great wild dahlia, its scarlet flowers drenched and heavy, sprawled over the hillside and an emerald-green grasshopper reclined on a petal, stretching its legs in the sunshine.

The dhabawallah was now up. His dog, emboldened by his master's presence, began to bark at us. The man lit a charcoal fire in a *choolah*, and put on it a kettle of water to boil.

'Would you like to eat something?' he asked conversationally in Hindi.

'No, just tea for us,' I said.

He placed two brass tumblers on a table.

'The milk hasn't yet been delivered,' he said. 'You're very early.'

'We'll take the tea without milk,' said Daljit. 'But give us lots of sugar.'

'Sugar is costly these days. But because you are schoolboys, and need more, you can help yourselves.'

'Oh, we are not schoolboys,' I said hurriedly.

'Not at all,' added Daljit.

'We are just tourists,' I lied unconvincingly.

'We have to catch the early train at Dehra,' offered Daljit.

'But there's no train before ten o'clock,' said the puzzled dhabawallah.

'It is the ten o'clock train we are catching!' said Daljit smartly. 'Do you think we will be down in time?'

'Oh yes, there's plenty of time . . .'

The dhabawallah poured out steaming hot tea into

the tumblers and placed the sugar bowl in front of us. 'At first I thought you were schoolboys,' he said with a laugh. 'I thought you were running away.'

Daljit almost gave us away by laughing nervously.

'What made you think that?' he asked.

'Oh, I've been here many years,' the dhabawallah replied, gesturing towards the small clearing in which his little wooden stall stood, almost like a trading outpost in a wild country. 'Schoolboys always pass this way when they're running away!'

'Do many run away?' I asked. I felt a little downcast at the thought that Daljit and I were not the first to embark on such an adventure.

'Not many. Just two or three every year. They get as far as the railway station in Dehra and there they're caught!'

'It is silly of them to get caught,' said Daljit disgustedly.

'Are they always caught?' I asked.

'Always! I give them a glass of tea on their way down, and I give them a glass of tea on their way up, when they are returning with their teachers.'

'Well, you won't be seeing *us* again,' said Daljit, ignoring the warning look that I gave him.

'Ah, but you aren't schoolboys!' said the shopkeeper, beaming at us. 'And you aren't running away!'

We paid for our tea and hurried on down the path. The parrots flew over again, screeching loudly, and settled in a lichee tree. The sun was warmer now, and, as the altitude decreased, the temperature and humidity rose and we could almost smell the heat of the plains rising to meet us.

The hills levelled out into the rolling countryside, patterned with fields. Rice had been planted out, and the sugarcane was waist-high.

The path had become quite slushy. Removing our shoes and wrapping them in newspaper, we walked barefoot in the soft mud. All these little out-of-routine acts simply added to our excitement and thrill, making everything quite unforgettable for life.

'It's about three miles into Dehra,' I said. 'We must go round the town. By now, everyone in school will be up and they'll have found out we've gone!'

'We must avoid the Dehra station then,' said Daljit.

'We'll walk to the next station, Raiwala. Then we'll hop onto the first train that comes along.'

'How far must we walk?'

'About ten miles.'

'Ten miles!' Daljit looked dismayed. 'It'll take us all day!'

'Well, we can't stop here nor can we wander about

in Dehra, neither can we enter the station. We have to keep on walking.'

'All right. We'll keep on walking. I suppose the beginning of an adventure is always the most difficult part.'

Soon, the fields were giving way to jungle. But there were still some fields of sugarcane stretching away from the railway lines.

'How much further do we have to walk?' asked Daljit impatiently. 'Is Raiwala in the middle of the jungle?'

'Yes, I think it is. We've covered about four miles I suppose. Six to go! It's funny how some miles seem longer than others. It depends on what one is thinking about, I suppose. If our thoughts are pleasant, the miles are not so long.'

'Then let's keep thinking pleasant thoughts. Isn't there a short cut anywhere? You've been in these forests before.'

'We'll take the fire-path through the jungle. It'll save us three or four miles. But we'll have to swim or wade across a small river. The rains have only just started, so the water shouldn't be too swift or deep.'

Heavy forests have paths cut through them at various places to prevent forest fires from spreading easily. These paths are not used much by people since they don't lead anywhere in particular, but they are frequently used by the larger animals.

We had gone about a mile along the path when we heard the sound of rushing water. The path emerged from the forest of sal trees and stopped on the banks of the small river I had mentioned earlier. The main bridge across the river stood on the main road, about three miles downstream.

'It isn't more than waist-deep anywhere,' I said. 'But the water is swift and the stones are slippery.'

We removed our clothes and tied everything into two bundles which we carried on our heads. Daljit was

a well-built boy, strong in the arms and thighs. I was slimmer. But I had quick reflexes.

The stones were quite slippery underfoot, and we stumbled, hindering rather than helping each other. We stopped in midstream, waist-deep, hesitating about going any further for fear of being swept off our feet.

'I can hardly stand,' said Daljit.

'It shouldn't get worse,' I said hopefully. But the current was strong, and I felt very wobbly at the knees.

Daljit tried to move forward, but slipped and went over backwards into the water, bringing me down too. He began kicking and thrashing about in fear, but eventually, using me as a support, he came up spouting water like a whale.

When we found we were not being swept away, we stopped struggling and cautiously made our way to the opposite bank, but we had been thrust about twenty yards downstream.

We rested on warm sand, while a hot sun beat down on us. Daljit sucked at a cut in his hand. But we were soon up and walking again, hungry now, and munching biscuits.

'We haven't far to go,' I said.

'I don't want to think about it,' said Daljit.

We shuffled along the forest path, tired but not discouraged.

Soon we were on the main road again, and there were fields and villages on either side. A cool breeze came across the open plain, blowing down from the hills. In the fields there was a gentle swaying movement as the wind stirred the sugarcane. Then the breeze came down the road, and dust began to swirl and eddy around us. Out of the dust, behind us, came the rumble of cart wheels.

'Ho! Heeyah! Heeyah!' shouted the driver of the cart. The bullocks snorted and came lumbering through the dust. We moved to the side of the road.

'Are you going to Raiwala?' called Daljit. 'Can you take us with you?'

'Climb up!' said the man, and we ran through the dust and clambered on to the back of the moving cart.

The cart lurched forward and rattled and bumped so much that we had to cling to its sides to avoid falling off. It smelt of grass and mint and cow-dung cakes. The driver had a red cloth tied round his head, and wore a tight vest and a dhoti. He was smoking a beedi and yelling at his bullocks, and he seemed to have forgotten our presence. We were too busy clinging to the sides of the cart to bother about making conversation. Before long we were involved in the traffic of Raiwala—a small but busy market town. We jumped off the bullock cart and walked beside it.

'Should we offer him any money?' I asked.

'No. He will be offended. He is not a taxi driver.'

'All right, we'll just say thank you.'

We called out our thanks to the cart driver, but he didn't look back. He appeared to be talking to his bullocks.

'I'm hungry,' declared Daljit. 'We haven't had a proper meal since last night.'

'Then let's eat,' I said. 'Come on, Daljit.'

We walked through the small Raiwala bazaar, looking in at the tea and sweet shops until we found the cheapest-looking dhaba. A servant-boy brought us rice and dal and Daljit ordered an ounce of ghee which he poured over the curry. The meal cost us two rupees but we could have as much dal as we wanted, and between us we finished four bowls of it.

'We'll rest at the station,' I said, as we emerged from the dhaba. 'We'll buy second-class tickets, and rest in the first-class waiting room. No one will check on us. We look first class, don't we?'

'Not after that walk through the jungle,' replied Daljit.

But we did occupy the best waiting room and Daljit made himself comfortable in an armchair. A train eventually came chugging in, and we were soon on our way to Delhi.

It didn't take us long to find a hotel once we got off at the Old Delhi Railway Station. It was called the Great Oriental Hotel, and was just behind the police station in Chandni Chowk. It didn't pretend to be even a third-class hotel, and for five rupees we were given a small back room which had a window overlooking the godown of an Afghan spice merchant. The powerful smell of asafoetida came up from the courtyard below.

We were tired and hot, so we tossed our belongings down on the floor and took turns at the bathroom tap. Then we stretched out on the only cot in the room and slept through the afternoon, oblivious to the noises from the street, the attentions of the insect population in the hotel mattress, and the creaking of the old fan overhead.

It was late evening when we woke up, and we were hungry again. Daljit opened the door and shouted. Presently a servant-boy appeared.

'Bring us tea, toast, two big omelettes, and a bottle of tomato sauce,' ordered Daljit with a confidence that I wished I had.

The omelettes, when they arrived twenty minutes

later, were tiny. Both had obviously been made from one egg. The sauce had been diluted with water, and the toasts were burnt. The salt was damp, and we had to prise open the salt-cellar to get to it. The pepper, however, came out in a generous rush and made up the major portion of the meal. As our hunger had not been satisfied by this poor fare, we ordered eggs again, boiled eggs this time. No matter how tiny, they would have to be whole.

'Let's go out,' said Daljit after we had eaten the eggs. 'It's stuffy in here.'

'I'm still sleepy,' I said.

'Then I'll go out for a little while. I may go to the gurdwara.'

'All right, but don't get lost.'

Drowsy, I closed my eyes, but the sounds of the city's unceasing traffic came through the window. Ships and distant ports seemed very far away but so did hills and mountain streams.

I fell asleep and woke up only when Daljit returned.

'I've solved our problem!' he said, beaming. 'We won't bother with the train. I met a truck driver, and he has offered to take us as far as Jaipur. That's more than a hundred miles. It will be quite safe to take a train from Jaipur.'

'When can your friend take us?'

'The truck leaves at four o'clock in the morning.'

'There's no rest for the wicked,' I said. 'Still, the less time we lose the better. It's Wednesday, and my uncle's ship might sail on Saturday. What will we have to pay?'

'Nothing. It's a free ride. The driver is a Sikh, and I persuaded him that we are related to each other through the marriage of my brother-in-law to his sister-in-law's niece!'

* * *

At four the next morning we made our way towards the Red Fort, its ramparts dark against the starry sky. The streets which had been teeming with so much life the previous evening were now deserted. The street lamps shed lonely pools of light on the pavements. The occasional car glided silently past, but it belonged to another kind of world altogether.

Near the Fort we found a couple of dhabas which were still open. They did business with the truck drivers who slept by day and drove by night.

Our driver, a tall, bearded Sikh, loomed over us out of the darkness. He had a companion with him, also a Sikh, who was still in his underwear.

'You can get in at the back,' said the driver in his

thick Punjabi which I could follow sufficiently well. 'We'll be off in a few minutes.'

The truck was parked beneath a peepul tree. We pulled ourselves up into the back of the open truck, only to find our way barred by what seemed at first to be a prehistoric monster.

The monster snorted once, stamped heavily on the boards, and sent us tumbling backwards.

'*Bhaiyyaji*!' cried Daljit to the driver. 'There's some kind of animal in here!'

'Don't worry, it's only Mumta,' said our friend.

'But what is it doing in here?'

'She is going with us. I am taking her to the market in Jaipur. So get in with her boys, and make yourselves comfortable.'

There was now enough light to enable us to take a closer look at our travelling companion. She was a full-grown buffalo from the Punjab.

'An excellent buffalo,' said Daljit, who appeared to be familiar with the finer points of these animals. 'Notice her blue eyes!'

'I didn't know buffaloes had blue eyes,' I said dryly.

'Only the best buffaloes have them,' said Daljit. 'Blue-eyed buffaloes give more milk than brown-eyed ones.'

Fortunately for us, the Sardarji started the truck and an early morning breeze, blowing across the river, swept away some of the stench so typical of buffaloes.

We were soon out of Delhi and bowling along at a fair speed on the road to Jaipur. The recent rain had waterlogged low-lying areas, and the herons, cranes and snipe were numerous. Fields and trees were alive with strange, beautiful birds: the long-tailed king crow, blue jays and weaver birds, and occasionally the great white-headed kite, which is said to be Garuda, Lord Vishnu's famous steed.

As we travelled further into Rajasthan, the peacocks became more numerous; so did the camels loping along the side of the road in straight, orderly lines. And, as the vegetation grew less and the desert took over, the people themselves grew more colourful, as though to make up for the absence of colour in the landscape. The women wore wide red skirts, and gold and silver ornaments. They were handsome, tall, fair and strong. The men were tall too and the older among them had flowing white beards.

As the day grew older, and the sun rose higher in the sky, the traffic on the road increased; but our truck driver, instead of slowing down, drove faster. Perhaps he was in a hurry to dispose of the buffalo. Soon he was trying to overtake another truck.

The truck in front was moving fast too, and its driver had no intention of giving up the middle of the road. It was piled high with stacks of sugarcane.

'It's going to be a race!' cried Daljit excitedly, standing up against the buffalo, in order to get a better view.

The road was not wide enough to take two large vehicles at once, and as the other truck wouldn't make way, ours had to fall in behind it, almost suffocating us with the exhaust fumes. We were thrown to the floorboards as the truck lurched over the ruts in the rough road, and Mumta, getting nervous, almost trampled upon us. Then there was a tremendous bump, a grinding of brakes, and we came to a stop.

As the dust cleared, we made out our driver's bearded face gazing anxiously down at us.

'Are you all right?' he asked gruffly.

'I think so,' I said.

'Did you overtake the other truck?' asked Daljit.

'No,' grunted our friend. 'He would not give way. You had better come in front.'

We agreed without any hesitation and his assistant rather grudgingly joined the buffalo.

After a few miles, the driver became friendly and told us that his name was Gurnam Singh.

It was getting dark by the time we reached Jaipur, so we were not able to see much of the city. We spent the night in the truck, sleeping in the back with Gurnam Singh. Mumta had been disposed of on the way. Jaipur nights can be chilly, even in summer, so Gurnam Singh considerately shared his bedding with us. Because he was accustomed to sleeping in the body of the truck, he was soon asleep, snoring loudly and rhythmically. Daljit and I tossed and turned restlessly. He kicked me several times in the night. The floor of the truck was hard, and retained various buffalo smells.

We had hardly fallen asleep (or so it seemed), when Gurnam Singh woke us up, saying that it was almost four o'clock and that he had to start on his return journey, this time with a load of red sandstone.

'What a life!' exclaimed Daljit, sleepily rubbing his eyes with one hand. 'I'd hate to be a truck driver.'

'One has to live somehow,' philosophized Gurnam Singh. 'I like driving. I knew how to drive when I was merely six or seven. The money is not so bad, either. Now, when I get back to Delhi, I will have two days off, which I will spend with my wife and children. Goodbye friends, and if you pass through Delhi again, you will find me near the walls of the Red Fort.'

We waved to him as he shot off in his truck, throwing up huge clouds of dust, making a great noise and probably waking the local inhabitants. Dogs barked, and a cock began to crow.

We were on the outskirts of the city, facing a large lake. On the other side was open country, bare hills and desert. We could also make out the ruins of a building—probably a palace or a hunting lodge—among some thorn bushes and babul trees.

'Let's go out there,' suggested Daljit. 'We can bathe in the lake and rest. Then later in the morning we can come into the city and find out about trains.'

We set out along the shores of the lake, and it was a good half-hour before we reached the opposite bank.

There was no one in the fields, but a camel was going round and round a well, drawing up water in small trays. Smoke rose from houses in a nearby village, and the notes of a flute floated over to us on the still morning air.

It took us about twenty minutes to reach the ruin, which seemed like an old hunting lodge put up by some Rajput prince when game must have been plentiful.

The gate of the lodge was blocked with rubble, but part of the wall had crumbled apart and we climbed through the gap and found ourselves in a stone-paved courtyard in the centre of which stood a dry, disused stone fountain. A small peepul tree was growing from the crack in the floor of the fountain. Finding nothing to do there, we made our way to the railway tracks again.

Daljit and I snuck on to a goods train. It was a hard night's journey. The train was agonizingly slow and stopped at many places. At one small station, a number of sacks filled with what must have been cattle-fodder were tossed into the wagon, almost burying us in our fitful sleep. But we found they were comfortable to rest on and lay stretched out on top of them until the first light of morning.

As the sky cleared, we knew we were not far from our journey's end. The landscape had undergone a complete change. We had left the desert for the coastal plain.

The tall waving palms parted, and then I spotted the sea.

It was the sea as I had always dreamt of it ever since my days in Kathiawar with my father. It was vast, lonely and blue, blue as the sky was blue, and the first ship I saw was a sailing-ship, an Arab dhow, listing slightly in the mild breeze that blew onto the shore.

The train stopped at a small bridge spanning a stream which wound its way across the plain down to the sea. We got down there and trudged the rest of the way to our destination.

Two hours later we were at Jamnagar.

We stopped near a small tea shop and watched other people eating laddoos and bhelpuri. We couldn't even afford a coconut.

'Where is the harbour?' I asked the shopkeeper.

'Two miles from here,' he replied.

'Are there any ships in the port?' I asked, relieved yet anxious.

'What do you want with a ship?'

'What does anyone want with a ship?'

'Well there's only one and it sails today, so you had better hurry if you want to go away on it.'

'Let's go,' said Daljit.

'Wait!' said a young man who was lounging against the counter. 'It will take you almost an hour to get there if you walk. I will take you in my cart.' He pointed to a shabby pony cart close by. The pony did not look as though it wanted to go anywhere.

'My pony is fast!' said the young man, following our glances. 'Never go by appearances. She may look tired but she runs like a champion! Get in friends, I will charge you only one rupee.'

'We don't have any money,' I said. 'We'll walk.'

'Fifty paisa, then,' he said. 'Fifty paisa and a glass of tea. Jump in my friends!'

'All right,' agreed Daljit. 'There's no time to lose. Fifty paisa and buy your own tea.'

We climbed into the cart, and the youth jumped up in front and cracked his whip. The pony lurched forward, the wheels rattled and shook, and we set off down the bazaar road at a tremendous trot.

'I didn't know you had fifty paisa left,' I said.

'I don't,' Daljit replied. 'But we'll worry about that later. Your uncle can pay!'

As soon as we were out of the town and on the open

road to the sea, the pony went faster. She couldn't help doing so, as the road was downhill. The wind blew my hair across my eyes, and the salty tang of the sea was in the air.

Daljit shook me in his excitement.

'We will soon be at the harbour,' he yelled joyfully. 'And then away at last!'

The driver called out endearments to his pony, and, exhilarated by the sea breeze and the comparative speed of his carriage, he burst into song. As we turned a bend in the road, the sea-front came into view. There were several small dhows close to the shore, and fishing-boats were beached on the sand. The fishermen were drying their nets while their children ran naked in the surf. A steamer stood out on the sea and though I could not make out its name from that distance, I was sure it was the *Iris*.

The cart stopped at the beginning of the pier, and we tumbled out and began running along the pier. But even as we ran, it became clear to me that the ship was moving away from us, moving out to the sea. Its propeller sent small waves rippling back to the pier.

'Captain!' I shouted. 'Uncle Jim! Wait for us!'

A lascar standing in the stern waved to us; but that was all. I stood at the end of the pier, waving my hands and shouting into the wind.

'Captain! Uncle Jim! Wait for us!'

Nobody answered. The seagulls, wheeling in the wake of the steamer, seemed to take up the cry—'Captain, Captain . . .'

The ship drew further away, gaining speed. And still I called to it in a hoarse, pleading voice. Yokohama, San Diego, Valparaiso, London, all slipped away for ever . . .

THE VANISHING TONGA

The tonga, the one-horse-drawn quick-moving and light vehicle, though still seen plying on roads in various parts of the country as a medium of transport, is losing fast its ground against scooters, motorcycles, cars and buses. The day is not far off when the tonga, once the undisputed 'king of vehicles', will disappear altogether from Indian roads.

I remember that when I was very young, I travelled all of thirty miles from Dehra Dun to Hardwar in a tonga. There were cars in those days—this was in the late 1940s—but a tonga was considered just as good, almost as fast, and certainly more dependable when it came to getting across the Song river in the dry season.

During the rains, when the river flowed strong and deep, it was impossible to get across except on a hand-operated ropeway (which is still used), but in the dry months, when the river was a trickle, the tonga horse went splashing through, the carriage wheels churning through the clear mountain water. If the horse found the going difficult, we removed our shoes, rolled up our pants, and waded across, the driver leading the horse by the muzzle.

Long before my time, in fact, before the turn of the century, when the 'Scinde Punjab and Delhi Railway' went no further than Saharanpur, the only way of getting to Dehra was by the 'night mail', better known as the *dak ghari*.

Dak ghari ponies were difficult animals, always attempting to turn around and get into the ghari with the passengers. It was only when the coachman used his whip liberally, and reviled the ponies' ancestors as far back as their third and fourth generations, that the beasts could be persuaded to move. And once they started, there was no stopping them; it was gallop all the way to the first stage, where the ponies were changed to the accompaniment of a bugle blown by the coachman in almost Dickensian fashion.

* * *

Besides the dak ghari, there was also the 'kart mel', a sort of two-wheeled pony cart. It could carry two passengers—one sat in front beside the driver, the other at the back beside the syce.

Travelling by dak ghari was by no means cheap. A full ghari was forty rupees for the trip; a single seat was twenty-five. Alternately, a seat in the mail cart could be had for eleven rupees. The distance was forty-nine miles.

If you preferred to spent the night at Saharanpur, and make the journey by day, there was the pleasure of driving through the Siwaliks, one of the loveliest ranges in the country.

The journey through the Siwaliks began—as it begins today—at the Mohand Pass. The ascent starts with a gentle gradient, which increases as the road becomes more steep and winding. The hills are abrupt and perpendicular on the southern side, but slope gently away to the north.

The first stage in the pass was Tunbara, under a huge rock on the right bank of the river. At the next stage, Landibara, the road became very steep, and it wasn't unusual to harness bullocks instead of ponies, in order to cover the distance to the tunnel driven through the crest of the hill from where the descent into the Dun commenced.

At this stage of the journey, drums were beaten, if it was day, and torches were lit, if it was night, because sometimes wild elephants resented the approach of this clumsy caravan, and trumpeting a challenge, would throw the bullocks into panic and confusion.

The Siwaliks, near Mohand, once so full of game, have now been denuded of their wealth. Shikaris have wiped out most of the animals, and timber merchants have ruined the forests. The dak ghari has given way to the tonga, and the tonga to the bus.

* * *

Today, it is the tonga that is nearing extinction. With the emergence of a prosperous middle class in many of our cities, the machine has been given preference as a form of conveyance. Scooters, motorcycles, cars, trucks, buses, ply on routes that were once the monopoly of tonga ponies and tramcars. Our roads, never built for such heavy traffic, are frequently cracking up.

Tongas are still to be seen in our towns, but they are confined to roads where taxis and buses do not penetrate; most tonga-drivers refuse to change with the times, and still ply their tongas, despite a diminishing income. Their ponies seem to have more traffic sense than some of our taxi drivers; they deal very well with traffic jams, seldom panic, and are involved in few accidents.

But give a tonga a straight stretch of clear road, and it will go into action, racing at breakneck speed, while its passengers cling to their seats for dear life, and the exhilarated driver cracks his whip, calls endearments to the pony, and breaks into the latest and most popular film song.

Tonga drivers vary according to the towns they belong to. In Lucknow, they are still courteous, garrulous, self-styled decendants of Nawabs. In Delhi—where you can see them only in the old city—they are aggressive and shrewd, matching the temper of the city. Many of them have sold their ponies and bought auto rickshaws. Everywhere, they are fading away.

Tongas, like tramcars, are becoming part of our nostalgia for the past. Good for the animal, perhaps. Though I have never met a tonga driver who starved his pony. And the greater the distance we put between our world and the world of animals, the less human we become.

And here's another fantasy journey I will never make: a leisurely tonga ride, over days, even weeks, from Dehra to Hardwar and on to Chandni Chowk in Delhi.

Plain Tales

BEER AT CHHUTMALPUR AND
OTHER SMALL-TOWN CHARMS

On the way back from Delhi, just outside the small market-town of Chhutmalpur, I am greeted by a large signboard above a small shop with just two words on it: COLD BEER. After a gruelling five-hour drive in the heat and dust of summer, a glass of chilled beer is welcome, so I ask the driver to stop. Otherwise I would have no reason to break my journey here.

Chhutmalpur is not the sort of place you would choose to retire in. It was last in the news when a young Dalit couple was burnt alive by their disapproving families. Only its Sunday market gives it some charm, when the varied produce of the rural interior finds its way on to the dusty pavements and the air is rich with noise, colour and odours. There are carpets of red chillies and stacks of grain, vegetables and seasonal fruits; bangles of lac and wooden artifacts; colourful underwear; cheap toys for the children; sweets of every description and churan to go with them. ('*Lakar hajam, patther hajam*!' cries the churan-seller. Digest wood, digest stones. When I tried the digestive pill, it appeared to be one part asafoetida and one part gunpowder.) Apart from this, Chhutmalpur has little to recommend it.

Which could also be said about Najibabad, where I stopped some forty years ago while on my way to Pauri-Garhwal. I was accompanying a friend to his village above the Nayar river. Getting there involved taking a train from Dehra Dun upto Luxor (across the Ganga), hopping on to another train, then getting off again at Najibabad and waiting for a bus to take us through the Tarai to Kotdwar, a little town in the foothills that seemed to lack any kind of character.

Najibabad must have been one of the least inspiring places on earth. Hot, dusty, apparently lifeless. We spent two hours at the bus stand—waiting for the bus driver who had gone missing—in the company of several donkeys, also quartered there. We were told that the area had once been the favourite hunting ground of a notorious dacoit, Sultana Daku, whose fortress overlooked the barren plain. I could understand him taking up dacoity—what else was there to do in such a place?—

and presumed that he looked elsewhere for his loot, for in Najibabad there was nothing worth taking. In due course he was betrayed and was hanged by the British, when they should instead have given him an OBE for stirring up the sleepy countryside.

It was close to noon before the missing bus driver turned up, a little worse for some late-night drinking. I could sympathize with him. If in 1940 Najibabad drove you to dacoity, in 1960 it drove you to drink.

Chhutmalpur and Najibabad are not unique. The genuine small town of the great plains is still a desperate place. The following lines I wrote about a town I visited briefly in the late 1950s could apply to any small town in UP or Bihar or Bengal:

'Every mohalla was congested and insanitary, and all the roads narrow and dusty...Near the masjid, I saw a gang of boys chase a terrified bow-legged dwarf. Two emaciated cows, that probably could no longer provide milk, roamed about in a state of semi-starvation. A group of eunuchs dressed in cheap silk ghagras strolled barefoot down the road, their long, gaunt faces made up with rouge and kajal. The jeering boys forgot about the dwarf and turned on them.

'Through my long walk I was followed by a

small, distracted goat. She stayed with me till I found a tonga, drawn by a lean, listless mare and driven by an ancient Muslim with a yellowing beard . . .

'At the bus stop there was confusion. Newly arrived passengers, looking sleepy and dishevelled, were surrounded on all sides by a sea of mud and rain water, while scores of tongas and cycle rickshaws jostled each other in trying to cater to them. As a result, only half the passengers found conveyances, while the other half found themselves ankle-deep in mud and garbage.'

And yet, during the time I stayed in a few such towns in my youth, barely making a living by my writing, I formed enduring bonds of friendship. Sometimes I found love. I met men and women of generous spirit, eccentric manner and great fortitude, all of whom have found their way into my stories.

Uninviting and unromantic on first acquaintance, these towns surprised me with small miracles: moonlight on quiet alleys past midnight, for instance. Or the scent of quenched earth and fallen neem leaves after the first rains. Or the happy riot of the weekly bazaar or a mela.

Romance lurks in the most unlikely places.

SHAHJAHANPUR

It is forty-five years since I last saw Shahjahanpur, a sleepy little town halfway between Delhi and Lucknow. I doubt if it has changed much. It wasn't the sort of place that changes. Even in 1960, when I stopped there for a few hours, it looked as though time had been standing still since the dramatic events of the 1857 uprising, which I described in my novella *A Flight of Pigeons*.

Forty years after those events, in 1896 to be exact, my father had been born in Shahjahanpur's 'military camp', according to Grandfather's army service records. Grandfather's regiment, the Scottish Rifles, must have been quartered there for a few months before moving on to Bareilly, Aligarh, Gorakhpur, Lucknow, and other cantonment towns across the hot and dusty Gangetic plains.

This was one reason for me to stop there, but I was also keen to visit the cantonment church, where he had probably been baptized, and where, during the outbreak of 1857, the European residents had been slaughtered. Among the few survivors were Ruth Labadoor and her mother. Their story came down to me from my father and other sources, and I was keen to follow it up.

The church was still there, of course, but locked up; a memorial to those who had been killed on that fatal day at the end of May stood in the parade ground (I believe it has since been removed); the mango groves and some old bungalows going back to Mutiny days were still evident; and crossing the little Khannant river was the bridge of boats which had played so important a part for those who were escaping from the town—first, the fleeing Europeans; later, the mutineers or their families when the British had retaken the district.

Founded in the seventeenth century, the town had a large Pathan population, and still does. The crowded city area and mohallas are still home to the descendants of Javed Khan, his friends and relatives, and those who had set fire to the cantonment bungalows. In his film of the story, *Junoon*, Shyam Benegal provided a rather opulent-looking Nawabi setting, but in reality Shahjahanpur's streets were occupied by working or lower-middle-class families, and only the Nawab (who lived elsewhere) would have enjoyed much affluence.

The dramatic events of 1857 led to the loss of many innocent lives on both sides of the conflict, Indian and British. In retelling Ruth's story I tried to show how the common humanity of ordinary folk—Hindu, Muslim, or Christian—could sometimes overcome the forces of hate, revenge and retribution.

On a lighter note: The Rose Rum factory stands a little way outside Shahjahanpur. It dates back to pre-Mutiny times. During the uprising it was sacked by rioters. Some quenched their thirst, while others poured barrels of good rum into the Khannant. Grandfather would have been appalled. I don't know if he was much of a drinker, but we did find these verses among his papers. He was, of course, referring to the Solan Brewery near Shimla. Like the Rosa distilleries, it is over 150 years old.

'Where's Solan?' the private was asking;
'Somewhere near Tibet, I should think.'
'There's a brewery there,
And it's brimming with beer,
But we can't get a mouthful to drink!'
So we route-march from Delhi to Solan
In the dust and the maddening sun,
And we're cursing away like Hades

Well knowing there ain't any ladies
To hear every son-of-a-gun!
And when we have climbed up to Solan
Our language continues profane,
For right well we know
We shall soon have to go
Down from Solan to Delhi again!

I'm not sure if Grandfather wrote the poem, but we'll credit it to him anyway—Henry William Bond, with a few profanities edited out by his grandson.

I should add that young Mr Carew, the proprietor of the Rosa distillery, went into hiding and survived the mutiny. If he had not done so, I would not be enjoying Carew's Gin today.

THE BREAK OF MONSOON
IN MEERUT

Crossing the Jamuna, still beautiful, before stretches of it came to resemble a huge nullah, the bus took us past a fast-expanding industrial area where a tractor factory was coming up next to a brewery. It was 1962, and I was travelling with my friend Kamal, the two of us having decided to see a bit of Uttar Pradesh. The bus took us across country where General Lake opposed the Maratha forces in 1803 and took Delhi for the British, and over the Hindon river and into UP.

Then north to Meerut, with green fields stretching out on either side: fields of maize, wheat and sugarcane, interspersed with mango orchards and plantations of floating lotus flowers, until we reached the outskirts of the ancient city, got down from the bus, stretched our limbs and climbed onto a cycle rickshaw with our cases and bedding-roll.

The rickshaw boy rode swiftly to the hotel, the only 'English hotel' in Meerut, a building which was probably a barracks at one time, and was owned and managed by a middle-aged Englishman whom we saw, once, when we blundered into the empty building. Apparently, it *wasn't* a hotel anymore, but Mr P had never bothered to take the signboard down, and if somebody did turn up, as we had done (this only happened about once a year), then they were welcome to a room and the services of his bearer and of course morning tea and breakfast.

Mr P, who lived alone with his wireless, opened a musty room for us and told us to call for the bearer if we needed anything, or wished to pay our bill. During our two-day stay we never saw him again; he did not emerge from his room, just next to ours; but we heard his radio whenever we cared to listen, mostly relaying BBC cricket commentaries.

Some eighteen miles from Meerut were the remarkable 'Christian' warrior princess Begum Samru's palace and cathedral (she had built both in the very early nineteenth century). We decided to visit them the next day. We took the same rickshaw—the boy attached himself to us for the remainder of our stay—into town on a day so hot and humid that the palace made little impression on me. What does stay in my memory is the restaurant that the rickshaw boy took us to that evening, in the Muslim quarter. It served excellent partridge curry (partridges were plentiful around Meerut) and kebabs. We bought two bottles of beer, which we drank on the veranda back in the hotel, to the crackle and hiss and vaguely military music issuing from Mr P's radio.

Monsoon broke the next day, and my memories of Meerut, ever since, have always been associated with the first rains.

There had been no rain at all for over a month, so the rickshaw boy had told us. Now there were dark clouds overhead, burgeoning with moisture. Thunder blossomed in the air. The dry spell was over. I knew it; the birds knew it; the grass knew it. There was the smell of rain in the air. And the grass, the birds and I responded to this odour with the same sensuous longing. I went out to the balcony, and waited.

A large drop of water hit the railing, darkening the thick dust on the woodwork. A faint breeze had sprung up, and again I felt the moisture, closer and warmer.

Then the rain approached like a dark curtain.

I could see it marching down the street, heavy and remorseless. It drummed on the corrugated tin roof and swept across the road and over the balcony. It swirled with the wind over the trees and roofs of Meerut.

Outside, the street emptied, The crowd dissolved in the rain. Then buses, cars and bullock carts ploughed through the suddenly rushing water. A garland of marigolds, swept off the steps of a temple, came floating down the middle of the road.

The rain stopped as suddenly as it had begun. The day was dying, and the breeze remained cool and moist. In the brief twilight that followed, I was witness to the great yearly flight of insects into the cool brief freedom of the night.

Termites and white ants, which had been sleeping through the hot season, emerged from their lairs. Out of every hole and crack, and from under the roots of trees, huge winged ants emerged, fluttering about heavily on this, the first and last flight of their lives. There was only one direction in which they could fly—towards the light, towards the street lights and the bright neon tubelight above the balcony.

This was the hour of the geckos, the wall lizards. They had their reward for weeks of patient waiting. Plying their sticky tongues, they crammed their stomachs, knowing that such a feast would not come their way again for a long time. Throughout the long hot season the insect world had prepared for this flight out of darkness into light, and the phenomenon would not happen again for another year.

Somewhere, an entire orchestra of frogs began their solemn music. The frogs woke great moths out of a slumber and they flew heavily into the balcony. I went in, shut the windows and got into bed thinking of fireflies flashing messages to each other in the mango groves outside Dehra.

A VAGABOND IN DELHI

I left Dehra for Delhi in 1959, and lived in the capital for a few years—freelancing, and for a time working with an international relief agency. I could not fall in love with Delhi, my heart was always in the hills and small towns of north India.

But there were things I came to like about Delhi, even in summer. The smell of a hot Indian summer is one smell that can never be forgotten. It is not just the thirsty earth with its distinctive odour, but all other ingredients of a hot weather in the plains that go to make this season almost intolerable on the one hand and sweetly memorable on the other. For who can forget that summer brings the jasmine, whose sweet scent drifts past us on the evening breeze along with the stronger odours and scents of mango blossom, raat-ki-rani and cowdung smoke.

Although I have spent most of my life in the hills. I grew up in some fairly hot places—humid Kathiawar ports, dusty old New Delhi, and the steamy Terai—and I am no stranger to prickly heat, mosquito bites, intermittent fever and dysentery and other hot-weather afflictions. Today's residents of the capital complain of pollution and overcrowding, and I wouldn't exchange my mountain perch for the pleasure of being fried crisp, but at least half of them have air conditioning, coolers, refrigerators and other means to keep the heat at bay. In 1940s' Delhi you were lucky to have a small table fan, and that was effective only if the bhisti, or water-carrier, came around with his goatskin bag, splashing water on to the khas-khas matting draped from your door or window; otherwise the fan simply blew hot air at you. I was in Delhi in the early '40s, living with my father, and I shall never forget the fragrant, refreshing smell of the wet khas-reed which cooled the rooms and verandas of New Delhi bungalows (the only high-rise building was the Qutab Minar).

My father and I lived in a small RAF hutment on the fringe of the scrub jungle near Humayun's tomb (a multi-storeyed hotel now occupies the site, and the jungle has been cleared to make way for the expensive residential area of Sunder Nagar). This was then furthest

Delhi, where one could expect to find peacocks in the garden and a snake in the bathroom. The bhisti and the khas-khas helped us to survive that summer. As did the box-like wind-up gramophone on which I played endless records which had to be stored flat in order to prevent them from warping and assuming weird shapes in the heat.

* * *

SILVER STREET, '59

One humid, uncomfortable September morning in 1959, I took the first bus into Chandni Chowk—Moonlight Square, or Silver Street. It set out from the historic Ajmere Gate, where old Delhi ends abruptly and 'Government' Delhi begins.

The bus took us past the great wide stretch of the Ramlila Grounds, where, at this early hour, there was considerable activity: young men in shorts and singlets sprinted about the ground; others, well-oiled and massaged, wrestled on the grass. Some played volleyball; others stood facing the sun, praying. There were also a few, further away, studying books, mumbling to themselves, or making speeches to invisible audiences, while all around them men scrubbed their teeth with neem twigs, bathed at the public tap, tied dhotis and turbans and prepared for the business of the long day that lay ahead.

Soon the sun would be up, government clerks would drink innumerable cups of tea (how like the English!), and the machinery of civilization and bureaucracy would run on as smoothly as ever.

We drove past the great walls of the Red Fort, Shah Jahan's palace, from the ramparts of which the Indian flag now fluttered in the breeze. Here Shah Jahan reigned in all the splendour of the Mughal Empire at the height of its power; and here an old Emperor, the last of the Mughals, lived in shabby poverty and wrote poetry, until the sepoys from Meerut made him a figurehead again.

Chandni Chowk was still the heart of Delhi in the late 1950s, as many of the markets of South and Central Delhi that are now popular with shoppers had not yet come up. It throbbed with vitality—even more alive than before with the advent of the enterprising Punjabi after Partition. The old buildings and landmarks were still there, the lanes and alleys as tortuous as ever, getting narrower as you went along, on foot or cycle-rickshaw, until the sky was almost shut out. Many of the shops were mere holes in the wall (as indeed they still are) and their wares spilled out on the pavement and across the tramlines—toys, silks and cottons, glassware, china, furniture, carpets and perfumes.

In front of the Municipal buildings the statue of Queen Victoria, which has since been removed, frowned upon the populace, as ugly as most statues, flecked with white pigeons' droppings. The pigeons, hundreds of them, sat on the railings and telephone wires, their drowsy murmurings muted by the sounds of the street, the cries of vendors and tonga drivers and the rattle of the tram.

The tram, now discontinued, was already a museum-piece. I do not think it had been replaced since it was first installed in the early twentieth century. It crawled along the crowded thoroughfare, clanging at an impatient five miles an hour, bursting at the seams with its load of people, while small children hung on by their toes and eyebrows.

Neither the tram nor the rickshaws appeared to bother an ash-smeared ascetic who sat at the side of the road and cooked himself a meal, or a hefty villager with a lotus flower tattooed on his forearm who stood in the middle of the street, staring at the Sunehri Masjid.

In the day of Shah Jahan, of course, Chandni Chowk would have been much wider and far less crowded. Historical records suggest that it was a wide avenue running from the Lahore Gate of the Red Fort to where the Fatehpuri Mosque still stands. In the middle of the avenue flowed a pleasant water-course. This channel from the West Jumna canal was built by Ali Mardan Khan to supply the palace with water; it gave the marketplace an attractive appearance, but in later years it was covered over, and nothing remains of it today.

A remarkable lady known as Begum Samru once lived in Chandni Chowk; her former residence, already lost behind a bank and a cinema in the fifties, is now a market for electrical goods. Begum Samru was originally a Kashmiri dancing-girl, who married the French adventurer Walter Reinhardt, known as Samru, or Sombre, because of his swarthy complexion. He came to India in 1750, and became the leader of a band of sepoys and European deserters. He fought for the Bharatpur Raja, and for Najaf Khan of Delhi, and it was from the latter that he received a grant of the Pargana of Sardhana, fifty-two miles from Delhi.

After Samru's death, his Begum succeeded to his domains. She became a Roman Catholic and built a cathedral near Sardhana, which still stands. Among her many lovers were the French adventurer Le Vaissoult, who committed suicide, and the Irish adventurer George Thomas, who for a few glorious years held kingdoms of his own at Hansi, Jhajjar and Karnal. He had on one occasion to make a dash from Jhajjar to Sardhana to rescue the Begum from her mutinous soldiers, who had chained her between two guns, placing her astride one of them at midday, when it was almost red-hot. Thomas got her out of this predicament, as he did from many others. She was none the worse for it, though, and survived other stormy episodes, to live to a ripe old age.

Chandni Chowk has often been called the richest street in Asia; it was not so long ago that great treasures were hidden away in the shops of curio dealers and jewellers. One of the most famous of these merchants was Messrs Kishan Chand and Sons, the firm that made the famous thousand-rupee 'Peacock Gown', which was worn by Lady Curzon at the Durbar Ball at the Delhi Fort in 1903, at which there were four thousand guests. Among the firm's treasures was a large black marble table, brought from Agra, where it had once been in the possession of Emperor Akbar.

Fifty, even thirty, years ago, you could strike up a conversation with any shop owner in Chandni Chowk, or a resident of the area trying to beat you to a rickshaw, and you would hear colourful legends about the place. In 2004, I was in the Silver Street again after more than thirty years, and confused by the crowds I asked for directions to Begum Samru's Palace. Three of the four people I asked had not heard of the Begum. The fourth directed me to a spanking new fast-food outlet!

* * *

WALKING THE STREETS OF NEW DELHI, '71

I settled down for good in Mussoorie in 1963, but of course I was to revisit Delhi many times, even spending a couple of winters there. On one of these visits, in 1971, I was staying at my friend Kamal's house in Rajouri Garden, a Punjabi colony in West Delhi. Needless to say, there were no gardens, and hardly any trees, and I would often wander off and spend almost the entire day in search of less depressing sights. One day I walked all the way to Connaught Place—a distance of eight miles— and back. When I mentioned this over dinner at night, the family greeted me with a bewildered silence.

Finally my friend's mother, a practical Punjabi lady, asked: 'How did you lose your money?' She kept hers knotted in the end of her sari, and believed that people who kept their money in easily snatched handbags and wallets were asking for trouble.

'I haven't lost anything,' I said.

'Aren't the buses running?'

'Oh, the buses are running. One nearly ran over me.'

'Then why did you walk?'

The consensus of opinion was that I was a little mad. They have never heard of anyone in Delhi walking from choice. They preferred to wait long periods for overcrowded buses, even if the distance to be covered was only a furlong.

But I was glad I had walked, though Delhi to me has always been one of the least attractive cities in which to walk about. There weren't even a tenth of the vehicles in the city thirty years ago than there are today, but crossing roads could still be hazardous. Single- and double-decker buses (many emitting smokescreens of diesel fumes), wildly driven taxis, unpredictable scooter-rickshaws, slow-moving Ambassador and Fiat cars and even slower tongas, and thousands of wavering, wayward cyclists made for chaos on the streets. On the main roads, cyclists were frequently knocked over and killed.

Setting out on my long walk that morning, I had realized that the pavement was meant for almost every purpose except walking. I was on the Najafgarh Road,

heading in the general direction of central Delhi. It was a straight road, but this was no straight walk. To find a thirty-yard stretch of unoccupied pavement was most unlikely. In a territory where every square foot of land had a high price, why should so much good pavement go to waste?

The first two wayside stalls belonged to sellers of lottery tickets. Theirs was a thriving business, perhaps much more than it is now, in the absence of television quizzes and game shows. All over Delhi, at almost every street corner, there was someone selling lottery tickets. The prizes were attractive enough. The owner of the winning ticket collected Rs 2,50,000—sometimes more— and there were a number of other prizes. And the income accruing to the state was also tremendous—so much so that almost every state in the country, including Delhi, had climbed on the lottery bandwagon. After all, it is easier than collecting taxes. No one, not even the street sweeper, grudged giving a rupee to the government if there was a chance in a million of his winning a fortune.

Not surprisingly, it was the rich businessman who often went in for lottery tickets in a big way, sometimes buying up forty or fifty tickets at a time. It was usually they who struck gold, not the poor, who could rarely, if ever, afford a ticket.

There was an extended family of Lohiawalas, a gypsy tribe of blacksmiths who had wandered into Delhi, camped on a pavement on Najafgarh Road, and were going about their ancient and traditional way of living. They were indifferent to the fast pace, the noise of traffic, the neon signs and Western clothes that surrounded them on all sides. Their bullock carts (in which they travelled and slept and had their babies and died) stood just off the pavement; these weree lined with old iron stamped with decorative patterns and studded with coloured stones.

A charcoal fire had been made in a hole in the ground, and this was kept alive by a bellows worked by a wheel turned by an attractive woman wearing a black blouse and black skirt. This sombre attire was set off by heavy silver anklets and a pair of very lively eyes. Another pair of bellows had been fashioned out of goatskin. A man was beating out a strip of red-hot tin on his anvil. A boy was filling a bent bicycle-pump with sand (to keep it firm) before straightening it out with his hammer. The entire family, including bearded old men, wizened old women ready to take off on broomsticks, and naked grandchildren, was at work. Handsome people, these; and although they lived in dirt and squalor, they seemed quiet and dignified.

A little farther along the road were some people
making what appeared to be straw mats. These turned
out to be roofs for the small shacks belonging to the
Rajasthani labourers who lived on the other side of an
open drain. The walls of these shacks were about four
feet high, the rooms about six feet square. There was no
sanitation; people used the drain. They bathed at a
public tap. During the rains, water moved sluggishly
along this drain, but now it was dry except for pools of
stagnant, slimy water, a grey liquid tinged with green. It

must have held treasures for anyone searching for biological specimens. (And indeed, the enterprising Delhiwala had not ignored this possibility, for further along, on Link Road, frogs were on sale to biology students.)

At this side of the road lay a dead pony, knocked down at night by a speeding truck. A portion had been eaten away by dogs and jackals. It was now being pecked at by crows; when the birds tired of the stinking carcass they moved on to a nearby fruit stall. No one seemed to notice this, least of all the fruit vendors. Well-dressed people passed by without a glance at dead horse or open drain. Was it apathy, or was it that Delhi people—city people—were unobservant by nature? Did city life dull the perceptions? Were the giant cinema hoardings so overpowering, so dazzling, that everything else paled into insignificance beside them? (How much worse it must be now!)

Some of the shack-dwellers had tried to make their homes attractive. They had whitewashed their walls, adorned them with crude but colourful drawings of birds and animals. But what a contrast there was between these humble homes and the elegant villas and bungalows of Kirti Nagar, Patel Road and Pusa Road, three prosperous areas of Delhi which lay on my route. A tenant had to pay anything from three to five hundred rupees a month for a tiny flat in one of those fine houses, and back then this was a princely sum.

It took me two hours of foot-slogging to finally reach Connaught Place, which was still the premier shopping centre of New Delhi. I remembered it well from my childhood, in the war years, and in 1971 it hadn't changed much. The milk bar I frequented as a boy was still there, although they did not sell milk any more; now it was espresso coffee and hamburgers. The Regal cinema had switched over to Hindi films. In its cellar was a discotheque. Shopfronts were more flashy, but service-lanes had not altered. And of course the faces and clothes were different. The British uniforms of the war years had given way to the uniforms of the hippies, who slouched about in beads and togas, unaccepted and even scorned by the local citizens. (Indians, and certainly the middle-class Punjabi, are not impressed by people who do not dress well!)

I was tired and hungry, and I lunched at a dhaba, one of many lining the outer pavements round Connaught Place. Outside, on the road, a small crowd had gathered round a turbaned Pathan. For a moment I feared violence to this exotic stranger; then I realized that the crowd was merely curious, even in good humour. The Pathan was extolling the virtues of an aphrodisiac mixture which he was trying to sell. 'Be happy!' he cried. 'And make your bulbul happy!'

In spite of the family-planning hoarding directly behind him, he appeared to be doing good business.

It was, after all, the marriage season.

I was forcibly reminded of this on my way back to Rajouri garden in the evening. The roads in and out of every other residential area were blocked by shamianas put up for marriage receptions. This was illegal, but the fine was a small one, and when a father was spending thousands on his daughter's wedding, he didn't mind paying a fine of forty rupees.

I found myself involved in a marriage procession on Pusa Road. It was impossible to get past the throng of people in the baraat, so I remained with them for some distance. If I chose to attend the reception, no one would turn me away. As most of the guests were seeing each other for the first time, it was possible for any well-dressed person to join the festivities. It was a colourful procession, headed by small urchin boys carrying gas lamps. After them came the bandwalas in red coats and white spats and Salvation Army caps, playing an admixture of military marches and popular Hindi film tunes of the sixties. Then the bridegroom's beautifully clothed friends and relatives. And finally the bridegroom, enthroned on top of a gaily caparisoned jeep.

I took a side road finally and left the procession, but found my way blocked by another marriage party. This time a heavily built Sikh, slightly tipsy, embraced me as a long-lost brother. He seemed to know me. Quite possibly I knew him when he was a smooth-cheeked lad of fifteen; but now, disguised by a magnificent beard, he reminded me of no one I have ever known. But he wanted me to join his party, and so, to humour him, I accompanied him for about a hundred yards, when he suddenly forgot me and rushed at some other old acquaintance.

I encountered another three processions, and four more shamianas, before I reached Rajouri Garden. I kept going by eating boiled eggs. These were sold on the roadside, sliced and served with pepper and salt on a piece of newspaper.

I was almost home. It did not look as though anyone in Delhi slept at night, but I was ready for bed.

But there was something I had to do first.

The seller of lottery tickets had been staring hopefully at me, and I hated to disappoint him last thing at night. So I produced a rupee and bought a ticket; and, in doing so, I felt that I had finally identified myself with the good people of Delhi.

* * *

STREET OF THE RED WELL

The sun beat down on the sweltering city of Old Delhi. Not a breath of air stirred in the narrow, winding streets. The old walled city, over three hundred years old, had no open spaces, no fountains, no sidewalks, no shady avenues. I had chosen what was quite possibly the hottest day in May, the temperature over 45° Celsius, to go walking in search of—what? A story, perhaps an adventure. Or that was what I set out to do. The heat of the day had willed otherwise.

I was, I think, the only one walking the streets from choice. Shopkeepers nodded drowsily beneath whirring ceiling fans. The pavement barber had taken his customer into the shelter of an awning. A fortune-teller had decided that there was nothing to predict and had fallen asleep under the same awning. A vegetable-seller sprinkled water on his vegetables in a dispirited fashion. Those cauliflowers were fresh an hour ago, they looked old already. Even the flies were drowsy. Instead of buzzing feverishly from place to place, they staggered about on tired legs.

It was the pigeons who had found all the coolest places. These birds had made the old city their own. New Delhi is for the crows who like to have a tree to sleep in, even if they take their meals from out of kitchens and verandas. But the pigeons prefer buildings, and the older the buildings the better. They are familiar with every cool alcove or shady recess in the crumbling walls of neglected mosques and mansions.

A fat, supercilious pigeon watched me now from the window ledge above a jeweller's shop. The pigeon's forebears settled here long before the British thought of taking Delhi. Conquerors had come and gone. Nadir Shah the Persian, Madhav Rao the Maratha, Chulam Kadir the Rohilla, and generations of goldsmiths and silversmiths. Hindus and Muslims had made and lost fortunes in the city, but nothing had disturbed the tranquil life of these pigeons. Their gentle cooing can always be heard when there is a lull in the jagged symphony of traffic noise. How do they manage to sound so cool?

But here was welcome relief for the human: a shady corner in Lal Kuan Bazaar (Street of the Red Well), where an old man provided drinking water to thirsty wayfarers such as myself. His water was stored in a surahi, an earthenware jug which keeps the water sweet and cool. I bent down, cupped my hands, and received the sparkling liquid as my benefactor tilted the surahi towards me.

Lal Kuan. The Red Well. Of course it was no longer here. But the street still bore its name. And I liked to think that here, in the middle of the street, where a bullock had gone to sleep, forcing the cyclists to make a detour, there was once a well made of dark red brick, where the water bubbled forth all day.

Imprisoned beneath the soil, held down by the crowded commercial houses of this old quarter, the water must still be there; it gave nourishment to an old peepul tree that grew beside a temple.

It was the only tree in the street. It jutted out from the temple wall growing straight and tall, dwarfing the two-storey houses. One of its roots, breaking through the ground, had curled up to provide a smooth, well-worn seat.

And it was cool here, beneath the peepul. Even when there was no breeze, the slender heart-shaped leaves revolved prettily, creating their own currents of air. No wonder the sages of old found it a good tree to sit beneath. No wonder they called it sacred.

On the other side of the road, a tall iron doorway was set in a high wall. Doors like this were only built in the nineteenth century, when a wealthy merchant's house had to be a miniature fortress as well as a residence. I could not see over the wall and I would have liked to know what lay behind the door. Perhaps a side-street, perhaps a market, perhaps a garden, perhaps . . .

The door opened, not easily, because it had been left closed for a long time, but slowly and with much complaint. And beyond the door there was only an empty courtyard, covered with rubble, the ruins of an old house. I was about to turn away when I hear a deep, tremendous murmur.

It was the cooing of many pigeons.

But where were they?

I advanced further into the ruin, and there, opening out in front of me, ready to receive me as the rabbit hole was ready to receive Alice, was an old, disused well.

I peered down into its murky depths. It was dark, very dark, down there; but that was where the pigeons lived, in the walls of this lost, long-forgotten well shut away from the rest of the city.

I could not see any water. So I dropped a pebble over the side. It struck the wall, and then, with a soft plop, touched water. At that instant there was a rush of air and a tremendous beating of wings, and a flock of pigeons, thirty or forty of them, flew out of the well, streaked upwards, circled the building, and then fell into formation, wheeled overhead, the sun gleaming white on their underwings.

I had discovered their secret. Now I knew why they always looked so cool, so refreshed, while we who walked the streets of Old Delhi did so with parched mouths and drooping limbs.

The pigeons are the only ones who still know about the Red Well.

FOOTLOOSE IN AGRA

(I went to Agra in 1965, to see the Taj. But what interested me about the city had little to do with Emperor Shah Jahan's grand monument to his love.)

The cycle rickshaw is the best way of getting about Agra. Its smooth gliding motion and leisurely rate of progress are in keeping with the pace of life in this old-world city. The rickshaw boy makes his way through the crowded bazaars, exchanging insults with tonga drivers, pedestrians and other cyclists; but once on the broad Mall or Taj Road, his curses change to carefree song and he freewheels along the tree-lined avenues. Old colonial-style bungalows still stand in large compounds shaded by peepul, banyan, neem and jamun trees.

Looking up, I notice a number of bright paper kites that flutter, dip and swerve in the cloudless sky. I cannot recall seeing so many kites before.

'Is it a festival today?' I ask.

'No, sahib,' says the rickshaw boy. 'Not even a holiday.'

'Then why so many kites?'

He does not even bother to look up. 'You can see kites every day, sahib.'

'I don't see them in Delhi.'

'Ah, but Delhi is a busy place. In Agra, people still fly kites. There are kite-flying competitions every Sunday, and heavy bets are sometimes placed on the outcome.'

As we near the city, I notice kites stuck in trees or dangling from electric wires; but there are always others soaring up to take their place. I ask the rickshaw boy to tell me something about the kite-fliers and the kitemakers, but the subject bores him.

'You had better see the Taj today, sahib.'

'All right take me to it. I can lunch afterwards.'

It is difficult to view the Taj at noon. The sun strikes the white marble, and there is a great dazzle of reflected light. I stand there with averted eyes, looking at everything—the formal gardens, the surrounding walls of red sandstone, the winding river—everything except the monument I have come to see.

It is there, of course, very solid and real, perfectly preserved, with every jade, jasper or lapis lazuli playing its part in the overall design; and after a while, I can shade my eyes and take in a vision of shimmering white marble. The light rises in waves from the paving-stones, and the squares of black and white marble create an effect of running water. Inside the chamber it is cool and dark but rather musty, and I waste no time in hurrying out again into the sunlight.

I walk the length of a gallery and turn with some relief to the river scene. The sluggish Yamuna winds past Agra on its way to its union with the Ganga. I know the

Yamuna well. I know it where it emerges from the foothills near Kalsi, cold and blue from the melting snows; I know it as it winds through fields of wheat and sugarcane and mustard, across the flat plains of Uttar Pradesh, sometimes placid, sometimes in flood. I know the river at Delhi, where its muddy banks are a patchwork of clothes spread out by the hundreds of washermen who serve the city and I know it at Mathura, where it is alive with huge turtles; Mathura, sacred city, whose beginnings are lost in antiquity.

And then the river winds its way to Agra, to this spot by the Taj, where parrots flash in the sunshine, kingfishers swoop low over the water and a proud peacock struts across the lawns surrounding the monument.

I follow the peacock into a shady grove. It is quite tame and does not fly away. It leads me to a small boy who is sitting in the shade of a tree, feasting on a handful of small green fruit.

I have not seen the fruit before, and I ask the boy to tell me what it is. He offers me what looks like a hard green plum.

'It is the fruit from the Ashok tree,' says the boy. 'There are many such trees in the garden.'

'Are you allowed to take the fruit?'

'I am allowed,' he says, grinning. 'My father is the head gardener.' I bite into the fruit. It is hard and sour but not unpleasant.

'Do you live here?' I ask.

'Over the wall,'he says. 'But I come here everyday, to help my father and to eat the fruit.'

'So you see the Taj Mahal every day?'

'I have seen it every day for as long as I can remember.'

'And I am seeing it for the first time . . . you're very lucky.'

He shrugs. 'If you see it once, or a hundred times, it is the same. It doesn't change.'

'Don't you like looking at it, then?'

'I like looking at the people who come here. They are always different. In the evening there will be many people.'

'You must have seen people from almost every country in the world.'

'That is so. They all come here to look at the Taj. Kings and Queens and Presidents and Prime Ministers and film stars and poor people too. And I look at them. In that way it isn't boring.'

'Well, you have the Taj to thank for that.'

He gazes thoughtfully at the shimmering monument.

His eyes are accustomed to the sharp sunlight. He sees the Taj every day, but at this moment he is really looking at it, thinking about it, wondering what magic it must possess to attract people from all corners of the earth, to bring them here walking through his father's well-kept garden so that he can have something new and fresh to look at each day.

A cloud—a very small cloud—passes across the face of the sun; and in the softened light I too am able to look at the Taj without screwing up my eyes.

As the boy said, it does not change. Therein lies beauty. For the effect on the traveller is the same today as it was three hundred years ago when Bernier wrote: 'Nothing offends the eye . . . No part can be found that is not skilfully wrought, or that has not its peculiar beauty.'

And so, for a few moments, this poem in marble is on view to two unimportant people—the itinerant writer and the gardener's boy.

We say nothing; there is really nothing to be said. (But now, a few months later, when I try to recapture the essence of that day, it is not the monument that I remember most vividly. The Taj is there of course; I still see it as a mirror for the sun. But what remain with me, more than anything else, are the passage of the river and the sharp flavour of the Ashok fruit.)

In the afternoon I walk through the old bazaars which lie to the west of Akbar's great red sandstone fort, and I am not surprised to find a small street which is almost entirely taken up by kite-shops. Most of them sell the smaller, cheaper kites, but one small dark shop has in it a variety of odd and fantastic creations. Stepping inside, I find myself face to face with the doyen of Agra's kite-makers, Hosain Ali, a feeble old man whose long beard is dyed red with the juice of mehendi leaves. He has just finished making a new kite from bamboo, paper and thin silk, and it lies outside in the sun, firming up. It is a pale pink kite, with a small green tail.

The old man is soon talking to me, for he likes to talk and is not very busy. He complains that few people buy kites these days (I find this hard to believe), and tells me that I should have visited Agra twenty-five years ago, when kite-flying was the sport of kings and even grown men found time to spend an hour or two every day with these dancing strips of paper. Now, he says, everyone hurries, hurries in a heat of hope, and delicate things like kites and daydreams are trampled underfoot. 'Once I made a wonderful kite,' says Hosain Ali nostalgically. 'It was unlike any kite seen in Agra. It had a number of small, very light paper discs trailing on a thin bamboo frame. At the end of each disc I fixed a sprig of grass, forming a balance on both sides. On the first and largest disc I painted a face and gave it eyes made of two small mirrors. The discs, which grew smaller from head to tail, gave the kite the appearance of a crawling serpent. It was very difficult to get this great kite off the ground. Only I could manage it.

'Of course, everyone heard of the Dragon Kite I had made, and word went about that there was some magic in its making. A large crowd arrived on the maidan to watch me fly the kite.

'At first the kite would not leave the ground. The discs made a sharp wailing sound, the sun was trapped in the little mirrors. My kite had eyes and tongue and a trailing silver tail. I felt it come alive in my hands. It rose from the ground, rose steeply into the sky, moving farther and farther away, with the sun still glinting in its dragon eyes. And when it went very high, it pulled fiercely on the twine, and my son had to help me with the reel.

'But still the kite pulled, determined to be free—yes, it had become a living thing—and at last the twine snapped, and the wind took the kite, took it over the rooftops and the waving trees and the river and the far hills for ever. No one ever saw where it fell. Sahib, are you listening? The Dragon Kite is lost, but for you I'll make a bright new poem to fly.'

'Make me one,' I say, moved by his tale, or rather by the manner of its telling. 'I will collect it tomorrow, before I leave Agra. Let it be a beautiful kite. I won't fly it. I'll hang it on my wall, and will not give it a chance to get away.'

It is evening, and the winter sun comes slanting through the intricate branches of a banyan tree, as a cycle rickshaw—a different one this time—brings me to a forgotten corner of Agra that I have always wanted to visit. This is the old Roman Catholic cemetery where so many early European travellers and adventurers lie buried.

Although it is quite probably the oldest Christian cemetery in northern India, it has none of that overgrown, crumbling look that is common to old cemeteries in monsoon lands. It is a bright, even cheerful place, and the jingle of tonga-bells and other street noises can be heard from any part of the grounds. The grass is cut, the gravestones are kept clean, and most of the inscriptions are still readable.

The caretaker takes me straight to the oldest grave—this is the oldest known European grave in northern India—and it happens to be that of an Englishman, John Mildenhall. The lettering stands out clearly:

> Here lies John Mildenhall, Englishman, who left
> London in 1599 and travelling to India through
> Persia, reached Agra in 1605 and spoke with the
> Emperor Akbar. On a second visit in 1614 he fell
> ill at Lahore, died at Ajmere, and was buried
> here through the good offices of Thomas
> Kerridge, Merchant.

During the seventeenth and eighteenth centuries, the
Agra cemetery was considered blessed ground by
Christians, and the dead were brought here from distant
places. Thomas Kerridge must have put himself to
considerable expense to bury his friend in Agra.
Mildenhall was a romantic, who styled himself an envoy
of Queen Elizabeth. Unfortunately he left no account of
his travels, although a couple of his letters are quoted in
the writings of Purchas, another English merchant, who
lies buried in the Protestant cemetery a couple of furlongs
away.

Nearby is the grave of the Venetian, Jerome Veronio,
who died at Lahore. According to some old records, he
had a hand in designing the Taj, modelling it on
Humayun's tomb in Delhi. There had for long been a
belief that this 'architect' of the Taj lay buried in the
cemetery but no one knew where. Then in 1945, Father

Hyacinth, Superior Regular of Agra, scraped the moss off a tombstone, revealing the simple epitaph: 'Here lies Jerome Veronio, who died at Lahore.'

Actually, there is no evidence that Veronio designed the Taj, and even if he had something to do with it, he was only one of a number of artists and architects who worked on its construction. The chief architect was Muhammed Sharif of Samarkand. Each drew a salary of one thousand rupees per month. Ismail Khan of Turkey was the dome-maker. A number of inlay workers, sculptors and masons were Hindus, including Manohar Singh of Lahore and Mohan Lal of Kanauj, both famous inlay workers.

A man of more authentic accomplishments was the Italian lapidary, Horten Bronzoni, whose grave lies at a short distance from Veronio's. He died on 11 August 1677. According to Tavernier, it was Bronzoni who cut the Koh-i-noor diamond; and, says Tavernier, he cut the stone very badly.

Bronzoni is again mentioned as having manufactured a model ship of war for Aurangzeb, who had been annoyed by the depredations of Portuguese pirates and was anxious to create a navy. The ship was floated in a huge tank and manoeuvred by a number of European artillerymen. It made a ridiculous sight and convinced the Emperor that a navy was out of the question.

There are over eighty old Armenian graves in the cemetery, but the only one that interests me is the tomb of Shah Azar Khan, an expert in the art of moulding a heavy cannon. One of these, 'Zamzamah', earned a measure of immortality in Kipling's *Kim*—who holds *Zam-Zammah*, that 'fire-breathing dragon', holds the Punjab, for the great green-bronze piece is always first of the conqueror's loot. The gun was 14.6 feet long, and is still at Lahore.

Other historic tombs lie scattered about the cemetery, but the most striking and curious of them is the grave of Colonel Jon Hessing, who died in 1803. It is a miniature Taj Mahal, built of red sandstone. Although small compared to a Mughal tomb, it is large for a Christian grave, and could easily accommodate a living family of moderate proportions. Hessing came to India from Holland, and was one of a colourful band of freelance soldiers (most of them deserters) who served in Sindhia's Maratha army. Hessing, we are told, was a good, benevolent man and a great soldier. The tomb was built by his wife Alice, who it must be supposed, felt as tenderly towards the Colonel as Shah Jahan felt towards his queen. She could not afford marble. Even so, her 'Taj' cost a lakh of rupees.

Outside, in the street, people move about with casual unconcern.

Street-vendors occupy the pavement, unwilling that their rivals should take advantage of a brief absence. In the banyan tree, the sparrows and bulbuls are settling down for the night. A kite lies entangled in the upper branches.

FLOWERS ON THE GANGA

RISHIKESH, 1961

'*Ganga mai ki jai*!' (Glory to Mother Ganga!)

Everyone raised the cry as the Hardwar bus moved out of Meerut. Most of the passengers, including Kamal and I, were going to take darshan of Mother Ganga. But while many were bound for Hardwar, we were going to Rishikesh, a more secluded templetown, situated on the banks of the Ganga at the point where the river emerges from the mountains and, hemmed in no longer by rocks and trees, stretches itself across the plains of Uttar Pradesh and Bihar, flowing past great cities like Kanpur, Allahabad, Benares and Patna, and into Bengal.

Just next to us sat a well-built woman with three small children. The eldest, a boy of about six, took a fancy to Kamal, and was soon lolling about on his knees.

In front of us, obliterating the view, sat a stout lala and his devoted wife. Lalaji proved to be an impatient and ill-tempered man. He quarrelled with the conductor, the driver and the ticket-seller. In order to travel in comfort he had reserved three front seats, but was unwilling to pay toll on the third seat which, he insisted, would only be occupied by his and his wife's feet. They gave in to him eventually. An urchin who inadvertently touched the sleeve of his kurta received a stinging slap. But he became more tolerant as time went on, and once, when engaged in an argument with a passenger at the other end of the bus, favoured me with a smile.

The countryside was monotonous up to Roorkee. Then the road took us along the Ganga canal, and Kamal sat up and began to look at things. We changed buses at Hardwar, and got into a very old and wheezy contraption which surprised us by going much faster than the government roadways bus. Probably the driver was trying to make up for time lost in stopping every five minutes to pick up some acquaintance on the road. We stopped for ten minutes at the Sat Narain temple, once famous for the tiger that used to visit it every evening. Rattling through the Motichur forest block, we saw two elephants—tame ones, possibly—and a variety of monkeys.

We left the bus at Rishikesh and went in search of my friend Jhardari, with whom we were to stay. He lived at Muni-ki-Reti, two miles upstream, where the wealthier ashrams were situated. His rooms, adjoining Swami Sivananda's Ashram, were on the right-hand bank of the Ganga.

Jhardhari was away, on a routine trip to Devprayag. As Secretary of the Tehri-Garhwal Motor Mazdoor Sangh Workers' Union, he has to travel all over the district to keep in touch with the men who drive the trucks and buses on the dangerous hill roads. The buses are privately owned; the government only nationalizes those services that use first-class roads. The state is very cautious about taking over the responsibility of transporting people to remote hill towns like Tehri and Pipalkoti, where pilgrims on the way to Gangotri or Badrinath must start their journey on foot. The motor roads in the interior are narrow, precipitous and unmetalled. To mention this is not to condemn them. Till a few years ago many of these regions had no roads at all. And Garhwalis are excellent drivers—many have experience of Army trucks—and serious accidents are uncommon.

Jhardhari's room-mate made us at home, and prepared hot, strong tea. Garhwalis drink more tea than Englishmen, and seldom take water. We were to become accustomed to drinking tea at almost hourly intervals.

One of the first things we did was to dip ourselves in the river. The water was icy cold, and it was impossible to stay in for more than ten minutes. Shivering, we climbed on to the bathing steps to dry ourselves. Our clothes felt hot against our bodies.

Down at the Rishikesh bathing ghat, hundreds of people would be dipping themselves in the sacred waters; but at Muni-ki-reti (which is in Tehri-Garhwal district, while the town of Rishikesh is in Dehra Dun district) there were only a few people by the river—a few pilgrims

from Bengal, Andhra and Madras; disciples from Swami Sivananda's Ashram; and a number of boys who work in the area.

Logs were always floating downstream, and boys would get across them, lying flat on their stomachs and paddling the planks through the water. Two of the more daring youths paddled their logs right across the river, to the temples on the opposite bank. They were good swimmers, but had they been parted from their floats they would have been carried away by the current and quite possibly drowned.

We walked down to Rishikesh in the evening, and saw over a hundred sadhus emerging from an ashram where they were given their evening meal. In their saffron robes, they flooded the dusty road, talking animatedly amongst themselves. Many of them were young men, probably novices. One was a strapping youth of about twenty, a Hercules gracefully wearing the robe of renunciation.

They looked well-fed and contented. Most of them spoke a little English. What had brought them to Rishikesh, I wondered, to live as recluses and ascetics? Personal tragedy, the stress of modern city life, or the failure of material pursuits . . . Or did the career of a religious mendicant hold out profitable prospects? Later on I was told that some of the novitiates should really have been in prison. But perhaps the rigours of their monastic existence rid them of early criminal tendencies; and if that was so, then surely ashrams were better places for them than jails.

Little shacks lined the river banks and though few people bathed late in the evening, hundreds were beside the water. Offerings of flowers in little leaf boats went sailing downstream. They were lighted by wicks dipped in oil, and went bobbing up and down on the water, sometimes for a considerable distance, until they were upset by rocks or inquisitive fish. Kamal sent an offering downstream, and requested Mother Ganga to grant him success as an artist. His boat, though, did not go very far. It came between the legs of a bather, an enormous Amazonian woman, and disappeared beneath her.

Undeterred, Kamal fed little balls of flour to the fish. They were huge, completely tame, and came to the bank in shoals to be fed by the bathers. Sometimes they fought amongst themselves, and a few of them were a raw pink where they had been savagely bitten.

That night we slept in the open, on a wide ledge above the riverbed. The lights from the temples and ashrams on the opposite bank reflected gently on the water. There was a *human* quietness everywhere. The sounds were of the river—the distant roar of the rapids, the nearby lapping of water on the bathing steps.

We bathed again in the river, as the sun came up over the mountain known as Manikoot Parbat. There is an unbroken ridge along the top of this mountain, stretching all the way to the snows of Badrinath, some two hundred miles away. Only a few hermits live on the mountain. It belongs to the elephants who sometimes visit the river in herds, to bathe and drink.

Jhardhari had returned, looking quite fresh after a 150-mile bus journey; and he offered to take us up to Narindernagar, a little town on a hilltop, which, though smaller and less central than Tehri, is the capital of the district. The former Maharaja had preferred it to the less congenial valley-town of Tehri on the banks of the Bhagirathi; and Narindernagar became the Maharaja's summer capital.

The buses were all full, and we had to travel up separately, one to each bus. First Kamal, then I, and last of all Jhardhari.

Narindernagar is only ten miles from Rishikesh, but it is also two thousand feet higher, and the bus has to climb a dizzy, winding road on which there can be no two-way traffic. But the buses go faster than their counterparts in the plains. With speedometers conveniently out of order, buses and trucks come downhill at a speed of thirty to thirty-five miles an hour. But, as I have said before, Garhwalis are very good drivers. Along the main highways of the Punjab are the wrecks of numerous trucks, some jammed up against trees, others in head-on collisions. But in the hills there is no driving at night, and the drivers prefer smoking bidis to drinking rum or country liquor. Mechanical failure is usually the cause of the few accidents that do occur.

From Narindernagar we went on for another eight miles, and eventually got down at Agra-khal, a pass in the mountains at a height of about five thousand feet. The motor road, soon becoming kaccha, continues to Tehri and Dharasu, and from the latter, pilgrims must proceed on foot to the shrines and temples of Gangotri.

After eating some hot puris, we walked back to Narindernagar, leaving the main road, and hiking through a forest of oak and pine. Kamal, who was seeing real mountains for the first time, was very excited and asked me innumerable questions about plants and streams and trees and rocks. He chattered away until Jhardhari said something flattering about his many and varied interests, and this embarrassed Kamal so much that he stopped talking altogether. I enjoyed the shade of the gnarled, untidy oaks, and the soft, slippery carpet of pine needles.

But after the forest there was bare hillside; the sun was scorching hot, and we had soon emptied the water bottle. So we rejoined the main road and stopped a truck going down to Rishikesh.

It was the first time Kamal and I had sat in the back of a truck travelling at speed down a mountain. It was impossible to anchor oneself on the floor. A kindly sadhu, also at the back, placed his blanket on a tyre and invited us to share it with him; but at every hairpin bend the tyre slid violently about the floor and we were

pitched off it. Kamal and I clung to each other to avoid being thrown against the sides of the truck; Jhardhari hung on to an iron bar; we were all feeling quite sick. Only the sadhu appeared unperturbed. He retained his seat on the tyre, even when it went skidding from one end of the truck to the other.

When we reached Rishikesh we went straight to the river. Never had Mother Ganga's waters been so refreshing. The giddiness disappeared. Then we lay down on the sand, and Kamal, like the sleepy giant Kumbhakarna in the Ramayana, did not come to life until it was time to eat.

We slept well that night. In the morning we would go to Lachhman Jhula and, passing the suspension bridge, walk a little way up Manikoot Parbat.

As the sun rose, turning the river to gold, we climbed into the boat that took pilgrims across to the temples on the other bank. The oarsmen sat in the prow, straining against the current, and the people in the boat raised the same ageless cry: '*Ganga mai ki jai*!'

Climbing ashore, we passed through groves of mango trees, planted by rich pilgrims for the benefit of the sadhus. Then, leaving behind Lachhman Jhula, we walked along the pilgrim route to Badrinath until we came to a dharamshala called Garur Chatti. Here we drank the inevitable but welcome tea, and set off up the hillside in search of a waterfall Jhardhari had told us about.

It did not take us long to reach the waterfall. Set amidst rocks and ferns, it fell about thirty feet onto a platform of smooth yellow rocks and pebbles. Here it formed a small pool, about waist deep, into which we leapt without hesitation. The water wasn't as cold as the Ganga's, and we could splash about for as long as we liked, while the waterfall sprayed down on our heads. The water was very clear and fresh, though it had a slightly bitter taste, evidence, I suppose, of a strong mineral content.

Further down the stream we found a lot of old bones, which Kamal insisted were the remains of a tiger's kill; indeed, they might have been, tigers having been seen on the mountain. But no tiger troubled us; only a band of langurs, swinging from tree to tree, seemed resentful of our presence and urged us to leave.

This we did at our leisure and, after more tea at Garur Chatti, and a visit to a small temple, where the courtyard floor was so hot to our bare feet that we had to skip about in agony, we trudged back to Muni-ki-Reti.

It was our last night sleeping beside the Ganga, and we rested with our chins in our hands, watching the river move silently past us, surging onward, India's lifeblood, inexorable and irresistible.

They say that if the Ganga ran dry, all life in India would cease. But, nourished by the eternal snows, it is the one river that can never run dry. As long as the mountains stand, the Ganga will flow to the sea, and millions will come to pay homage to its holy waters.

* * *

HARDWAR, 1963

Flowers floating down the river: yellow and scarlet cannas, roses, jasmine, hibiscus. They are placed in boats made of broad leaves, then consigned to the waters with a prayer. The strong current carries them swiftly downstream, and they bob about on the water for fifty, sometimes a hundred yards, before being submerged in the river. Do the prayers sink too, or do they reach the hearts of the many gods who have favoured Hardwar—'Door of Hari, or Vishnu'—these several hundred years?

The river issues through a gorge in the mountains with a low booming sound. It does not break its banks until it levels out over the flat plains of Uttar Pradesh and Bihar. It is fast and muddy; but this does not deter thousands from descending the steps of the bathing-ghats, and plunging into the cold, snow-fed waters. For the Ganga washes away all sin.

Says the Mahabharata: 'To repeat her name brings purity, to see her secures prosperity, to bathe in or drink her waters saves seven generations of our race . . . There is no place of pilgrimage like the Ganga, no god like Vishnu . . .'

Almost every child knows the story of how the Ganga descended from heaven. For a thousand years King Sagara's great grandson stood with his hands upraised, praying for water to enable him to make the funeral oblations for the ashes of his 60,000 grand-uncles. Almost all the gods were involved in the affair. Finally, when the waters of the Ganga were released from heaven and the river reached the earth, the prince mounted his chariot and drove towards the spot where the ashes of his kinsmen lay. Wherever he went, the Ganga meekly followed. Gods, nymphs, demons, giants, sages, and great snakes, all joined in the procession, and as the river followed in the footsteps of the prince, the whole multitude of created beings bathed in her sacred waters and washed away their sins.

The multitude that followed the prince could be the same multitude that throngs the riverfront today. I see

no one who is not delighted at the prospect of entering the water. '*Ganga mai ki jai*!' The cry goes up mostly from the older people who have come here, many for the last time, to make their peace with the gods. Only their ashes will make the trip again.

It is a big crowd, although this is just an ordinary day of the week and not an occasion of special religious significance. Every day is a good day for bathing in the Ganga. But at the time of major festivals, such as Baisakhi, elaborate arrangements have to be made, including special trains and police reinforcements, to take care of the great influx of pilgrims. The number of pilgrims at the Baisakhi festival usually exceeds 1,00,000. During the Kumbh Mela, held every twelve years, there may be as many as 5,00,000 present on the great bathing-day. This is ten times the normal population of Hardwar. And when one realizes that the town is bounded by the steep Siwalik hills on one side and the river on the other, and has one main street leading to the riverfront, it is not surprising that in the past large numbers of people were crushed to death in stampedes at the narrow entrance to the ghats.

Fortunately the main street is a broad and pleasant thoroughfare. Although Hardwar is ancient (the Chinese traveller, Hiuen Tsang, records a visit made in the seventh century), little remains of earlier settlements. There are only two or three old temples. But the present buildings— tall, balconized structures put up in the 1920s and 1930s— have a certain old-world charm. Even new houses follow the same pattern. This isn't conscious planning; it is simply that Hardwar is a conservative town and clings to its traditions.

Most of the buildings along the road are dharamsalas. The road is shaded by tall old peepul and banyan trees. In some places the trees reach right across the street to touch the roofs of the three-storey buildings on the other side. At several places I find small peepul saplings growing out of the walls of buildings. One young peepul has sprung up in the fork of an adult kadam tree and will probably throttle it in time. No one fells the sacred peepul. It is better that walls should crumble or kadam trees wither. At least this guarantees the survival of one species of tree in a world where forests are rapidly disappearing.

To fell a peepul is to invite trouble; for the tree is the abode of spirits, and the man who cuts so much as a branch is likely to be pursued by all the spirits he had disturbed.

Peepuls live for hundreds of years, and Hardwar's oldest trees must have been here before the present town reached maturity. Some will be as old as the eleventh-century Mayadevi temple, which is probably the oldest temple in Hardwar. On a sultry day there can be no pleasanter spot than the shade of a peepul tree; the leaves are perpetually in motion, even when there is no breeze, and spin around in currents of their own making. It is no wonder that the man who plants a peepul is blessed by generations of Hindus to come.

While I stand beneath one of these giant trees, a devout and elderly man approaches with a watering-can, and, circling the tree, waters the soil around the base of the trunk. I move out of the way of his sprinkler watching the ritual in some surprise. It has been raining steadily for some days, and the tree should have no need of water.

'Why are you watering it?' I ask.

'Why does one water anything?' asks the old man. 'So that it may grow and flourish, of course.'

'But it's been raining almost every day.'

'Rain is something else,' he says. 'I am not responsible for the rain. This is water from the Ganga, and I have fetched it myself. That makes a lot of difference.'

I cannot argue. He waters the tree with love; and his love for the tree, as much as rain-water or river-water, is what makes it flourish.

Leaving the main street, I enter the bazaar.

The Hardwar bazaar is a long, narrow, winding street, probably the oldest part of the town, and free of all vehicular traffic. The road is no more than four yards wide. The small shops are spilling over with sweets, pickles, bead-necklaces, sacred texts, ritual designs, festival images, and pictures of the gods in vibrant colours. There is something in these naive, gaudy prints that acts as a transformer, making the more abstract Hindu philosophies comprehensible to anxious farmer or acquisitive taxi driver.

The bazaar winds and turns back upon itself, and eventually I find myself back at the river-front, gazing out across the river at the forested foothills. Few of the pilgrims on the bathing-steps can realize that sometimes at night a tiger stands on the opposite bank watching the bright illuminations of the temples, or that elephants listen to the rumbling of the trains bringing pilgrims to Hardwar from all parts of India.

It is evening now, and there are fewer people at the ghats. Most of the bathers are family people—farmers and small shopkeepers with their wives and children and aged parents. One does not see many students, or young people in Western clothes. Hardwar is old-fashioned, and so are most of the people who come here.

Charity, too, is old-fashioned, and Hardwar thrives on charity: donations to the temples and alms to the beggars, mendicants and itinerant ash-smeared sadhus. The beggars do not follow one about, as in the larger cities. They are confident of receiving coins from the pilgrims who pass by on the steps to the river. They simply sit there, occasionally calling out, but preferring to listen to the music of small coins dropping into brass begging-bowls.

Close by are the money changers, squatting before baskets which are brimming over with small change. In the rest of the country there is a shortage of small coins, and shopkeepers often decline to provide change; but in Hardwar you can change any number of notes for small coins. You are going to leave all the coins here anyway, when you distribute it along the river-front.

As the pilgrims leave the ghats, the joy of having accomplished their mission bursts forth in songs of praise: 'Henceforth no more pain, no more sickness; all will be well in future; *Ganga mai ki jai*!'

At Home in the Hills

THE TRAIL TO THE BANK

Local residents have got fed up with offering me lifts on the road to our hilltop bank and post office. They typically drive up the steep road to Landour in third (or is it fourth?) gear, see me plodding along on foot, and out of the goodness of their hearts, stop and open the door for me.

Although I hate to disappoint them, I close the door, thank them profusely, and insist that I am enjoying my walk. They don't believe me, naturally; but with a shrug, the drivers get into gear again and take off, although sometimes they have difficulty getting started, the hill being very steep. As I don't wish to insult them by reaching the bank first, I sit on the parapet wall and make encouraging sounds until they finally take off. Then I renew my leisurely walk up the hill, taking note of the fact that the wild geraniums and periwinkles have begun to flower and that the whistling thrushes are nesting under the culvert over which those very cars pass every day.

Many people—car drivers anyway—think I'm a little eccentric. So be it. I probably am eccentric! But having come to the Himalayan foothills forty years ago in order to enjoy *walking* among them, I am not about to stop now, just because everyone else has stopped walking. The hills are durable in their attractions, and my legs have proved durable too, so why should we not continue together as before?

Now, I'm no fitness freak. I don't jog either. If I did, I would almost certainly miss the latest wildflower to appear on the hillside, and I would not be able to stop awhile and talk to other people on the road—villagers with their milk and vegetables, all-weather postmen, cheeky schoolchildren, inquisitive tourists—or to exchange greetings with cats, dogs, stray cows and runaway mules. (Runaway mules are friendly creatures except towards their owners. I chat with the owners too, when they come charging up the road. I try to put them in good humour, so as to save the mules from a beating.)

Most of these people I have mentioned are walkers from necessity. Those who walk for pleasure grow fewer by the day. I don't mean long-distance trekkers or high altitude climbers, who are almost professional in their approach to roads and mountains. I mean people such as myself who are not great athletes but who enjoy sauntering through the woods on a frosty morning, leaving the main road and slithering downhill into a bed of ferns, or following a mountain stream until you reach the small spring in the rocks where it begins . . .

It takes a car less than five minutes up the hill to get to the bank. It takes me roughly twenty-five minutes. But there is never a dull minute. Apart from having interesting animal and human encounters, there are the changes that occur almost daily on the hill slopes: the ferns turning from green to gold, the Virginia creepers becoming a dark crimson, horse chestnuts falling to the ground.

On today's walk I spot a redstart, come down early from higher altitudes to escape the snow. He whistles cheerfully in a medlar tree. Wild ducks are flying south. There they go, high over the valley, heading for the lakes and marshlands.

If there's no one on the road, and I feel like a little diversion, I can always sing. I don't sing well, but there's no one to hear me except for a startled woodpecker, so I can go into my Nelson Eddy routine, belting out the songs my childhood gramophone taught me. 'Tramp, Tramp, Tramp', 'Stouthearted Men', 'Song of the Open

Road'! No one writes marching songs now, so I have to rely on the old ones.

Above me the blue sky, around me the green forest, below me the dusty plains.

Presently I am at Char-Dukaan—'Four Shops'—and the bank and post office.

Letters posted, I enter the bank, to be greeted effusively by the manager, Vishal Ohri—not because I have come to make a large deposit, but because he is that rarity among bank managers, a nature lover! When he learns that I have just seen the first redstart of the winter, he grows excited and insists that I take him to it. As we are nearing the office tea break, he sets off with me down the road and, to our mutual satisfaction and delight, is still in the medlar tree, putting on a special performance seemingly for our benefit.

The manager returns to his office, happy to be working at this remote hilltop branch. Both staff and customers will find him the most understanding and sympathetic of managers today, for has he not just seen the first white-capped redstart to fly into Landour for the winter? That's as good a 'first' as any in those books of records.

As long as there are nature-loving bank managers, I muse on my way home, there's still hope for this little old world. And for bank depositors, too!

HILL OF THE FAIRIES

Fairy Hill, or Pari Tibba as the paharis call it, is a lonely uninhabited hill, almost a mountain, lying to the east of Mussoorie, at a height of about 6000 feet. Some nights I have seen a greenish light zigzagging about the hill. Is this 'fairy light' what gives the hill its name? No one has been able to explain it satisfactorily to me; but often from my window I see this strange light.

I have visited Pari Tibba occasionally, scrambling up its rocky slopes where the only paths are the narrow tracks made by goats and the small hill cattle. Rhododendrons and a few stunted oaks are the only trees on the hillsides, but at the summit is a small, grassy plateau ringed by pine trees.

It may have been on this plateau that the early settlers tried building their houses. All their attempts met with failure. The area seemed to attract the worst of any thunderstorm, and several dwellings were struck by lightning and burnt to the ground. People then confined themselves to the adjacent Landour hill, where a flourishing hill station soon grew up.

Why Pari Tibba should be struck so often by lightning has always been something of a mystery to me. Its soil and rock seem no different from the soil or rock of any other mountain in the vicinity. Perhaps a geologist can explain the phenomenon; or perhaps it has something to do with the fairies.

'Why do they call it the Hill of the Fairies?' I asked an old resident, a retired schoolteacher. 'Is the place haunted?'

'So they say,' he said.

'Who say?'

'Oh, people who have heard it's haunted. Some years after the site was abandoned by the settlers, two young runaway lovers took shelter for the night in one of the ruins. There was a bad storm and they were struck by lightning. Their charred bodies were found a few days later. They came from different communities and were buried far from each other, but their spirits hold a tryst every night under the pine trees. You might see them if you're on Pari Tibba after sunset.'

There are no ruins on Pari Tibba, and I can only presume that the building materials were taken away for use elsewhere. And I did not stay on the hill till after sunset. Had I tried climbing downhill in the dark, I would probably have ended up as the third ghost on the mountain. The lovers might have resented my intrusion; or, who knows, they might have welcomed a change. After a hundred years together on a windswept mountain-top, even the most ardent of lovers must tire of each other.

Who could have been seeing ghosts on Pari Tibba after sunset? The nearest resident is a woodcutter who makes charcoal at the bottom of the hill. Terraced fields and a small village straddle the next hill. But the only inhabitants of Pari Tibba are the langurs. They feed on oak leaves and rhododendron buds. The rhododendrons contain intoxicating nectar, and after dining—or wining—to excess, the young monkeys tumble about on the grass in high spirits.

The black bulbuls also feed on the nectar of the rhododendron flower, and perhaps this accounts for the cheekiness of these birds. They are aggressive, disreputable little creatures, who go about in rowdy gangs. The song of most bulbuls consists of several pleasant tinkling notes; but that of the Himalayan black bulbul is as musical as the bray of an ass. Men of science, in their wisdom, have given this bird the sibilant name of *Hypsipetes psaroides*. But the hillmen, in their greater wisdom, call the species the *ban bakra*, which means the 'jungle goat'.

Perhaps the flowers have something to do with the fairy legend. In April and May, Pari Tibba is covered with the dazzling yellow flowers of St. John's Wort (wort meaning herb). The paharis call the flower a wild rose, and it does resemble one. In Ireland it is called the Rose of Sharon. In Europe this flower is reputed to possess certain magical and curative properties. It is believed to drive away all evil and protect you from witches.

Can St. John's Wort be connected with the fairy legend of Pari Tibba? It is said that most flowers, when they die, become fairies. This might be especially true of St. John's Wort.

There is yet another legend connected with the mountain. A shepherd boy, playing on his flute, discovered a beautiful silver snake basking on a rock. The snake spoke to the boy, saying, 'I was a princess once, but a jealous witch cast a spell over me and turned me into a snake. This spell can only be broken if someone who is pure in heart kisses me thrice. Many years have passed, and I have not been able to find one who is pure in heart.' Then the shepherd boy took the snake in his arms, and he put his lips to its mouth, and at the third kiss he discovered that he was holding a beautiful princess in his arms. What happened afterwards is anybody's guess.

There are snakes on Pari Tibba, and though they are probably harmless, I have never tried taking one of them in my arms. Once, near a spring, I came upon a checkered water snake. Its body was a series of bulges. I used a stick to exert pressure along the snake's length, and it disgorged five frogs. They came out one after the other, and, to my astonishment, hopped off, little the worse for their harrowing experience. Perhaps they, too, were enchanted. Perhaps shepherd boys, when they kiss the snake-princess, are turned into frogs and remain inside the snake's belly until a writer comes along with a magic stick and releases them from bondage.

Biologists probably have their own explanation for the frogs, but I'm all for perpetuating the fairy legends of Pari Tibba.

A WAYSIDE TEA SHOP

The Jaunpur range in Garhwal is dry, brown and rocky. Water is hard to find, and green fields are to be seen only far down in the valley, near the Aglar or some smaller stream. Elsewhere only monsoon crops are grown.

I have walked five miles without finding a spring or even a shady spot along the sun-blistered path, and I am beginning to wonder if the only living creatures in the area are the big lizards, who slither about on the hot surface of the rocks and stare at me with unwinking eyes. Just as I am asking myself if it is better to be a lizard than a thirsty trekker, I round a bend and discover a small mountain oasis: a crooked little shack tucked away in a cleft of the hillside. Growing beside the shack is a single pine tree, humming softly in the faint breeze that drifts across the mountains.

When one tree suddenly appears in this way, lonely

and dignified in the midst of a vast treeless silence, it can be more beautiful than a forest.

There is no glamour about the shack, a loose stone structure with a tin roof held down by stones. But it is a tea shop, one of those little pockets of pioneering mankind that spring up in the mountain wilderness to serve the weary traveller. Go where you will in Garhwal, you will always find a tea shop to sustain you just when you feel you have reached the end of your tether.

A couple of mules are tied to the pine tree, and the mule drivers, handsome men in tattered clothes, sit on a bench in the shade, drinking tea from brass tumblers. The shopkeeper, a man of indeterminate age—the cold dry winds from the snows have crinkled his face like a walnut but his teeth are sound and his eyes are clear— greets me as a long-lost friend, although we are meeting for the first time.

As a concession to my shirt and trousers, he produces a chair for me. It is a period chair, possibly even a Sheraton, but the stuffing has come out of the seat. It must have escaped from the nearby hill station of Mussoorie, where the sahibs foregathered in years gone by. The shopkeeper apologizes for its condition: 'The rats have been nesting in it.' And then, to reassure me, 'But they have gone now.'

I would just as soon be on the bench with the mule drivers, but do not wish to offend the shopkeeper, who has already given me his name, Megh Chand, and taken mine. So I take his chair into the shade and gently lower myself into it.

'Do you live here alone?' I ask.

'Sometimes I am alone,' he says. 'My family is down in the village, looking after the fields. It is quite far, six miles. So I go home once a week, and then my son comes up to look after the shop.'

'How long have you had the shop?'

'Oh, ten-fifteen years, I do not remember exactly.'

Why bother to count the years? In remote mountain areas, time has a different meaning; you may count the days, but not the hours. And yesterday, today, and tomorrow merge into one long day. When there is nowhere to go, you have no need of a clock. You eat when you are hungry, and sleep when you are tired.

But the mule drivers have somewhere to go and something to deliver—pumpkins and potatoes. They are busy men of the world, and presently they lead their pack-animals away down the dusty path.

'Tea or lassi?' Megh Chand gives me a choice, and I take the lassi, which is sharp and refreshing. The wind sighs gently in the upper branches of the pine tree and

I relax in my Sheraton chair like some eighteenth-century nabob who has brought his own chair into the wilderness.

Megh Chand tells me that he has been starved of good conversation. 'Next year,' he says, sitting down on the steps of his shop, 'the government will be widening the road, and then the buses will be able to stop here. For many years I have depended on the mule drivers, but they do not have much money to spend. Once the buses come, I will have many customers. Then perhaps I can afford to go to Delhi to have my operation.'

'What operation?'

'Oh, a *rasoli* (a growth) in my stomach. Sometimes the pain is very bad. I went to the hospital in Mussoorie, but they told me I would have to go to Delhi for an operation. Whenever someone is seriously ill, they say, "Go to Delhi"! Does the whole world go to Delhi to get treated? My uncle was told to go to Delhi for an operation. He went from one hospital to another until his money was finished, and then he came back to the village and died within a week. So maybe I won't go for the operation. The money is needed here. Once the buses come, I will have to keep sweets and biscuits and other things, and also a boy to help me cook a few meals. All I can offer you today is a bun. It was made in Delhi, I am told.'

'I'd rather have your lassi than a Delhi bun,' I

protest, for the bun looks as old as the Sheraton chair.
'But where do you get your water?' I ask.

'Come, I will show you,' he says, and takes me
round to the back of the shack and through an unexpected
gap in the hillside. It gives me a breathtaking glimpse of
snow-clad mountains striding into the sky. It is cool and
shady on the northern face of the hill, and here, issuing
from a rock, is a trickle of water. Yellow primulae grow
in clusters along the edges of a damp, dripping rock-
face. The water collects in a small stone trough.

'There is no other *cheshma* (spring) along this road,'
he says, 'and the buses can't go down into the ravine,
unless they fall into it. So they will have to stop here!' He
is triumphant.

We return to the shop front, where a milkman has
just arrived with a container of milk. He too sits down
for rest, refreshment and conversation. Next year, if the
road is ready (and it is a big 'if', because with hill roads
you can never be sure), and if he can afford the fare (an
even bigger 'if'), the milkman will be able to use the bus.
But there are some who will walk anyway, because they
have always been walking. Or ride mules, because they
have been doing it all their lives.

Still, when the road comes, time will take on new
dimensions for Megh Chand. Even in remote mountain

areas, buses must keep to some sort of schedule, and Megh Chand will have to be sure that his pot is on the boil, and be on the lookout for arrivals and departures. He will be better off than he is today but he is aware that prosperity has its pitfalls. He remembers a cousin, who opened a small grocery shop on a new bus-route near Devprayag. One day, some young hooligans got off the bus, looted his shop, and left him battered and bruised. It was the sort of thing that had never happened before . . .

It is time for me to be on my way. I leave Megh Chand and his Sheraton chair with regret.

'I hope the road will soon be ready,' I say in parting. 'I hope you will make lots of money. I hope you will be able to go to Delhi for your operation. And I hope I can come this way again.'

Hillman or plainsman, we have only our hopes to keep us going.

MEETINGS ON THE TEHRI ROAD

The human personality can impose its own nature on its surroundings. At a dark, windy corner in the bazaar, one always found an old man hunched up over his charcoal fire, roasting peanuts. He died one summer a couple of years back.

Then, some weeks later, there was a new occupant of the corner, a new seller of peanuts. No relative of the old man; but a boy of thirteen or fourteen, cheerful, involved, exchanging good-natured banter with his customers. In the old man's time it seemed a dark, gloomy corner. Now it's lit up by sunshine: a sunny personality, smiling, chattering. Old age gives way to youth; and I'm glad I won't be alive when the new peanut-vendor grows old. One shouldn't see too many people grow old.

Leaving the main bazaar behind, I walk some way down the Mussoorie–Tehri road, a fine road to walk on,

in spite of the dust from an occasional bus or jeep. From Mussoorie to Chamba, a distance of some thirty-five miles, the road seldom descends below 7000 feet, and there is a continual vista of the snow ranges to the north and the valleys and rivers to the south. Dhanolti is one of the lovelier spots, and the Garhwal Mandal has a rest-house here, where one can spend an idyllic weekend. Some years ago I walked all the way to Chamba, spending the night at Kaddu-khal, from where a short climb takes one to the Sirkhanda Devi terhple.

If one were to leave the Tehri road, one can trek down to the little Aglar river and then up to Nag Tibba, 9000 feet, which has a good oak forest and animals ranging from barking-deer to Himalayan bear. But this is an arduous trek and you must be prepared to spend the night in the open or seek the hospitality of a village.

Having wandered some way down the Tehri road, it is quite late by the time I return to the Landour bazaar. Lights still twinkle on the hills, but shop fronts are shuttered and the little bazaar is silent. The people living on either side of the narrow street can hear my footsteps, and I can hear their casual remarks, music, a burst of laughter.

Through a gap in the rows of buildings I can see Pari Tibba outlined in the moonlight. A three-quarter moon is up, and the tin roofs of the bazaar, drenched with dew, glisten in the moonlight. Although the street is unlit, I need no torch. I can see every step of the way. I can even read the headlines on the discarded newspaper lying in the gutter.

Although I am alone on the road, I am aware of the life pulsating around me. It is a cold night, doors and windows are shut; but through the many chinks, narrow fingers of light reach out into the night. Who could still be up? A shopkeeper going through his accounts, a college student preparing for his exams, someone coughing and groaning in the dark.

Three stray dogs are romping in the middle of the road. It is their road now, and they abandon themselves to a wild chase, almost knocking me down.

The rickshaw stand is deserted. One rickshaw catches the eye because it is decorated with dahlias and marigolds, most of them still fresh.

A jackal slinks across the road, looking right then left—he knows his road-drill—to make sure the dogs have gone. A field rat wriggles through a hole in a rotting plank on its nightly foray among sacks of grain and pulses.

Yes, this is an old bazaar. The bakers, tailors, silversmiths and wholesale merchants are the grandsons of those who followed the mad sahibs to this hilltop in the 1830s and 1840s. Most of them are plainsmen, quite prosperous even though inany of their houses are crooked and shaky.

Although the shopkeepers and tradesmen are fairly prosperous, the hill people—those who come from the surrounding Tehri and Jaunpur villages—are usually poor. Their small holdings and rocky fields do not provide them with much of a living, and men and boys have often to come into the hill station or go down to the cities in search of a livelihood. They pull rickshaws, or work in hotels and restaurants. Most of them have somewhere to stay.

But as I pass along the deserted street, under the shadow of the clock tower, I find a boy huddled in a recess, a thin shawl wrapped around his shoulders. He is wide awake and shivering.

I pass by, head down, my thoughts already on the warmth of my small cottage only a mile away. And then I stop. It is almost as though the bright moonlight has stopped me, holding my shadow in thrall.

> *If I am not for myself,*
> *Who will be for me?*
> *And if I am not for others,*
> *What am I*
> *And if not now, when?*

The words of an ancient sage beat upon my mind. I walk back to the shadows where the boy crouches. He does not say anything, but he looks up at me, puzzled and apprehensive. All the warnings of well-wishers crowd in upon me—stories of crime by night, of assault and robbery. But this is not Northern Ireland or Lebanon or the streets of New York. This is Landour in the Garhwal

Himalayas. And the boy is no criminal. I can tell from his features that he comes from the hills beyond Tehri. He has come here looking for work and he has yet to find any.

'Have you somewhere to stay?' I ask. He shakes his head; but something about my tone of voice has given him confidence, because now there is a glimmer of hope, a friendly appeal in his eyes.

I have committed myself. I cannot pass on. A shelter for the night—that's the very least one human should be able to expect from another.

'If you can walk some way,' I offer, 'I can give you a bed and blanket.'

He gets up immediately—a thin boy, wearing only a shirt and part of an old track-suit. He follows me without any hesitation. I cannot now betray his trust. Nor can I fail to trust him.

So now there are two in the sleeping moonlit bazaar. I glance up at the tall, packed houses. They seem to lean towards each other for warmth and companionship.

The boy walks silently besides me. Soon we are out of the bazaar and on the footpath. The mountains loom over us. A fox dances in the moonlight and a night-bird calls. And although no creature of the forest has ever harmed me, I am glad to have a companion as I walk towards another Himalayan dawn.

THE ROAD TO ANJANI SAIN

Fog, mist, cloud, rain, and mildew—these were the things the British must have looked for when selecting suitable sites for the hill stations they set up in the Himalayan foothills 150 years ago: Simla, Mussoorie, Darjeeling, Dalhousie, Nainital, all soggy with monsoon or winter mist and dripping oaks and deodars. The climate must have reminded them of their homes on the English moors or the Scottish highlands.

I have survived all that through the forty or so mountain monsoons that have been thrown at me; and having gone through the annual ritual of wiping the mildew from my books and a certain green fungus from my one and only suit, I decided some years ago to leave cloud country behind for a few days and be the guest of Cyril Raphael, at the Bhuvneshwari Mahila Ashram (a social service organization), at Anjani Sain in Tehri-Garhwal.

Pine country this, dry and bracing, with the scent of pine resin in the air. I have always thought 5000 to 6000 feet a healthier altitude to live at, but perhaps I'm prejudiced, having been born in Kasauli, which is pine rather than deodar country. Anjani Sain is about the same height and gets the sun all day. Given adequate food and pure water, it's a healthy place to live. Contrary to what most people think, Garhwal is not a poverty-stricken area. Almost everyone has a bit of land and does at least have the traditional *do-roti* for sustenance, which is more than can be said for the urban unemployed in other parts of northern India. But medical facilities are certainly lacking.

This area has always been known as Khas-patti, probably because it was special in several ways—climate-wise and probably economy-wise too. Down in the flat valley, there are green fields and even mango trees, the descent to lower altitudes being quite sudden in these parts. The small Anjani Sain bazaar, with its single bank, post office, and chemist's shop, shimmers in the noon sun; it looks like a set for a gunfight like in old westernsl. But this is, generally, a peaceful area.

At the ashram, I am in time for an early lunch—thick rotis made from *mandwa* (millets)—two of these are more than enough for me! Endless glasses of milky tea will see me through till supper time.

Towering over Anjani Sain, and blessing all those who live or pass beneath, is the Chanderbadni temple, dedicated to one of the incarnations of the goddess Parvati. As this is not one of the main pilgrim routes, the temple does not get as many visitors as some of the other sacred shrines in the hills. Below the Chanderbadni peak is a rest-house, for those who wish to break their journey here.

Anjani Sain lies midway between Tehri and Devprayag—a two-hour bus ride from either place. I came via Tehri, the road climbing steeply above the hot, dusty town that is destined to be submerged by the waters of the Tehri Dam. The dam should have been ready by now, but having been the subject of a great deal of controversy, work on it has progressed in fits and starts.

I am told that this entire region is 'eco-fragile', one of those words bandied around at seminars all, over the world. Well, I am not an expert in these matters, (and who is, I wonder?) but I should think most of our earth is 'eco-fragile', having had to put up with hundreds of thousands of years of human civilization.

Do we stop all development in the name of preserving the environment? Or do we move on regardless? *Proceed with caution* would be the rational person's answer. But are human beings really rational?

Old Tehri was no beauty spot, and New Tehri (growing rapidly above it), is even uglier; from a distance it looks like a giant cemetery.

When the architecture of suburban Delhi is brought to the hills, what is there to say? You just look the other way.

Fortunately the defaced mountain is soon left behind, and as it slips out of sight and we ascend into the pine regions, the eye is soothed by the pretty, slate-covered houses of the villages and their little gardens ablaze with marigolds and yellow and bronze chrysanthemums.

Chrysanthemums love this climate. Down in the fields there are patches of crimson *cholai* (amaranth) interspersed with the fresh green of young wheat.

And here be leopards! My companion tells me of one that strolls down the motor road every evening, forcing the local bus to go around him. His presence also accounts for the absence of stray dogs.

Suddenly in the distance I see what at first glance appears to be a cloud or a large white sailing ship. On approaching, it turns out to be the freshly white-washed buildings of the Bhuvneshwari Mahila Ashram, clinging to the steep slopes of the mountain.

Here, for two or three days, I find rest and sustenance. The manifold activities of the ashram, (directed mainly towards the welfare of widows and small children) are there for all to see, and I recall the relief work undertaken by its young field workers after the Uttarkashi earthquake last year—they had rushed to the area before the government agencies could swing into action.

However, as a social worker I am somewhat inept. I am just a frazzled old writer who now seeks a refuge from the all-pervasive clutter of tourism that makes ordinary life almost impossible in our hill stations.

I hope the land-grabbers and the real estate 'developers' never get this far. They are welcome to their malls and artificial lakes and concrete parks. Just so long as I am free to escape from it all, to sit here at Anjani Sain contemplating a large white rose in Cyril's garden, while the rest of the world watches video.

WHERE RIVERS MEET

It's a funny thing, but long before I arrive at a place I can
usually tell whether I am going to like it or not.

Thus, while I was still some twenty miles from the
town of Pauri, I felt it was not going to be my sort of
place; and sure enough, it wasn't. On the other hand,
while Nandprayag was still out of sight, I knew I was
going to like it. And I did.

Perhaps it's something on the wind—emanations of
an atmosphere—that are carried to me well before I
arrive at my destination. I can't really explain it, and no
doubt it is silly to make judgements in advance. But it
happens and I mention the fact for what it's worth.

As for Nandprayag, perhaps I'd been there in some
previous existence, I felt I was nearing home as soon as
we drove into this cheerful roadside hamlet, some little
way above the Nandakini's confluence with the
Alakananda river. A *prayag* is a meeting place of two

rivers, and as there are many rivers in the Garhwal Himalayas, all linking up to join either the Ganga or the Jamuna, it follows that there are numerous prayags, in themselves places of pilgrimage as well as wayside halts en route to the higher Hindu shrines at Kedarnath and Badrinath. Nowhere else in the Himalayas are there so many temples, sacred streams, holy places and holy men.

Some little way above Nandprayag's busy little bazaar, is the tourist rest-house, perhaps the nicest of the tourist lodges in this region. It has a well-kept garden surrounded by fruit trees and is a little distance from the general hubbub of the main road.

Above it is the old pilgrim path. Just over twenty years ago, if you were a pilgrim intent on finding salvation at the abode of the gods, you travelled on foot all the way from the plains, covering about two hundred miles in a couple of months. In those days people had the time, the faith and the endurance. Illness and misadventure often dogged their footsteps, but what was a little suffering if at the end of the day they arrived at the very portals of heaven? Some did not survive to make the return journey. Today's pilgrims may not be lacking in devotion, but most of them do expect to come home again.

Along the pilgrim path are several handsome old houses, set among mango trees and the fronds of the papaya and banana. Higher up the hill the pine forests commence, but down here it is almost sub-tropical. Nandprayag is only about 3000 feet above sea level—a height at which the vegetation is usually quite lush provided there is protection from the wind.

In one of these double-storeyed houses lives Mr

Devki Nandan, scholar and recluse. He welcomes me into his house and plies me with food till I am close to bursting. He has a great love for his little corner of Garhwal and proudly shows me his collection of clippings concerning this area. One of them is from a travelogue by Sister Nivedita—an Englishwoman, Margaret Noble, who became an interpreter of Hinduism to the West. Visiting Nandprayag in 1928, she wrote:

> Nandprayag is a place that ought to be famous for its beauty and order. For a mile or two before reaching it we had noticed the superior character of the agriculture and even some careful gardening of fruits and vegetables. The peasantry also suddenly grew handsome, not unlike the Kashmiris. The town itself is new, rebuilt since the Gohna flood, and its temple stands far out across the fields on the shore of the Prayag. But in this short time a wonderful energy has been at work on architectural carvings, and the little place is full of gem-like beauties. Its temple is dedicated to Naga Takshaka. As the road crosses the river, I noticed two or three old Pathan tombs, the only traces of Mohammedanism that we had seen north of Srinagar in Garhwal.

Little has changed since Sister Nivedita's visit, and there is still a small and thriving Pathan population in Nandprayag. In fact, when I called on Mr Devki Nandan, he was in the act of sending out Id greetings to his Muslim friends. Some of the old graves have disappeared in the debris from new road cuttings: an endless business, this road-building. And as for the beautiful temple described by Sister Nivedita, I was sad to learn that it had been swept away by a mighty flood in 1970, when a cloudburst and subsequent landslide on the Alakananda resulted in great destruction downstream.

Mr Nandan remembers the time when he walked to the small hill station of Pauri to join the old Messmore Mission School, where so many famous sons of Garhwal received their early education. It would take him four days to get to Pauri. Now it is just four hours by bus. It was only after the Chinese invasion of 1962 that there was a rush of road-building in the hill districts of northern India. Before that, everyone walked and thought nothing of it!

Sitting alone that same evening in the little garden of the rest-house, I heard innumerable birds break into song. I did not see any of them, because the light was fading and the trees were dark, but there was the rather melancholy call of the hill dove, the insistent ascending trill of the koel, and much shrieking, whistling and twittering that I was unable to assign to any particular species.

Now, once again, while I sit on the lawn surrounded by zinnias in full bloom, I am teased by that feeling of having been here before, on this lush hillside, among the pomegranates and oleanders. Is it some childhood memory asserting itself? But as a child I never travelled in these parts.

True, Nandprayag has some affinity with parts of the Doon valley before it was submerged by a tidal wave of humanity. But in the Doon there is no great river running past your garden. Here there are two, and they are also part of this feeling of belonging. Perhaps in some former life I did come this way, or maybe I dreamed about living here. Who knows? Anyway, mysteries are more interesting than certainties.

Presently the room-boy joins me for a chat on the lawn. He is in fact running the rest-house in the absence of the manager. A coach-load of pilgrims is due at any moment but until they arrive the place is empty and only the birds can be heard. His name is Janakpal and he tells me something about his village on the next mountain, where a leopard has been carrying off goats and cattle. He doesn't think much of the conservationists' law protecting leopards: nothing can be done unless the animal becomes a man-eater!

A shower of rain descends on us, and so do the pilgrims. Janakpal leaves me to attend to his duties. But I am not left alone for long. A youngster with a cup of tea appears. He wants me to take him to Mussoorie or Delhi. He is fed up, he says, with washing dishes here.

'You are better off here,' I tell him sincerely. 'In Mussoorie you will have twice as many dishes to wash. In Delhi, ten times as many.'

'Yes, but there are cinemas there,' he says, 'and television, and videos.' I am left without an argument. Birdsong may have charms for me but not for the restless dish-washer in Nandprayag.

The rain stops and I go for a walk. The pilgrims keep to themselves but the locals are always ready to talk. I remember a saying (and it may have originated in these hills), which goes: 'All men are my friends. I have only to meet them.' In these hills, where life still moves at a leisurely and civilized pace, one is constantly meeting them.

Into the Mountains

GREAT RIVERS OF THE MOUNTAINS

THE GANGA DESCENDS

There has always been a mild sort of controversy as to whether the true Ganga (in its upper reaches) is the Alaknanda or the Bhagirathi. Of course the two rivers meet at Deoprayag and then both are Ganga. But there are some who assert that geographically the Alaknanda is the true Ganga, while others say that tradition should be the criterion, and traditionally the Bhagirathi is the Ganga.

I put the question to my friend Dr Sudhakar Misra, from whom words of wisdom sometimes flow; and, true to form, he answered: 'The Alaknanda is the Ganga, but the Bhagirathi is Gangaji.'

One sees what he means. The Bhagirathi is beautiful, almost, caressingly so, and people have responded to it with love and respect, ever since Shiva released the waters of the goddess from his tangled locks and she sped plains-wards in the tracks of Prince Bhagirath's chariot.

He held the river on his head,
And kept her wandering, where,
Dense as Himalayas woods were spread,
The tangles of his hair.

Revered by Hindus, and loved by all, the goddess Ganga weaves her spell over all who come to her. Moreover, she issues from the very heart of the Himalayas. Visiting Gangotri in 1820, the writer and traveller Baillie Fraser noted: 'We are now in the centre of the Himalayas, the loftiest and perhaps the most rugged range of mountains in the world.'

Perhaps it is this realization that one is at the very centre and heart of things, that gives one an almost primeval sense of belonging to these mountains and to this river valley in particular. For me, and for many who have been in the mountains, the Bhagirathi is the most beautiful of the four main river valleys of Garhwal. It will remain so provided we do not pollute its waters and strip it of its virgin forests.

The Bhagirathi seems to have everything—people of

a gentle disposition, deep glens and forests, the ultravision of an open valley graced with tiers of cultivation leading up by degrees to the peaks and glaciers at its head.

From some twenty miles above Tehri, as far as Bhatwari, a distance of about fifty-five miles along the valley, there are extensive forests of pine. It covers the mountains on both sides of the river and its affluents, filling the ravines and plateaus up to a height of about 5000 feet. Above Bhatwari, forests of box, yew and cypress commence, and if we leave the valley and take the roads to Nachiketa Tal or Dodi Tal—little lakes at around 9000 feet above sea level—we pass through dense forests of oak and chestnut. From Gangnani to Gangotri the deodar is the principal tree. The excelsa pine also extends eight miles up the valley above Gangotri, and birch is found in patches to within half a mile of the glacier.

On the right bank of the river, above Sukhi, the forest is nearly pure deodar, but on the left bank, with a northern aspect, there is a mixture of silver-fir, spruce and birch. The vally of the Jad-ganga is also full of deodar, and towards its head the valuable pencil-cedar is found. The only other area of Garhwal where the deodar is equally extensive is the Jaunsar-Bawar tract to the west.

It was the valuable timber of the deodar that attracted the adventurer Frederick 'Pahari' Wilson to the valley in the 1850's. He leased the forests from the Raja of Tehri in 1859, and in a few years, he had made a fortune.

The old forest rest-houses at Dharasu, Bhatwari and Harsil were all built by Wilson as staging-posts, for the only roads were narrow tracks linking one village to another. Wilson married a local girl, Gulabi, from the village of Mukhba, and the portraits of Mr and Mrs Wilson (early examples of the photographer's art) still hang in these sturdy little bungalows. At any rate, I found their pictures at Bhatwari. Harsil is now out of bounds to civilians, and I believe part of the old house was destroyed in a fire a few years ago.

Amongst other things, Wilson introduced the apple into this area, and 'Wilson apples'—large, red and juicy— are sold to travellers and pilgrims on their way to Gangotri. This fascinating man also acquired an encyclopaedic knowledge of the wildlife of the region, and his articles, which appeared in *Indian Sporting Life* in the 1860s, were later plundered by so-called wildlife experts for their own writings.

Bridge-building was another of Wilson's ventures. These bridges were meant to facilitate travel to Harsil and the shrine at Gangotri. The most famous of them was a 350-foot suspension bridge over the Jad-ganga at Bhaironghat, over 1200 feet above the young Bhagirathi where it thunders through a deep defile. This rippling contraption of a bridge was at first a source of terror to travellers, and only a few ventured across it. To reassure people, Wilson would often mount his horse and gallop to and fro across the bridge. It has long since collapsed but local people will tell you that the hoofbeats of Wilson's horse can still be heard on full moon nights! The supports of the old bridge were complete tree-trunks, and they can still be seen to one side of the new motor-bridge put up by engineers of the Northern Railway.

Wilson's life is fit subject for a romance; but even if one were never written, his legend would live on, as it has done for over a hundred years. There has never been any attempt to commemorate him, but people in the valley still speak of him in awe and admiration, as though he had lived only yesterday. Some men leave a trail of legend behind them, because they give their spirit to the place where they have lived, and remain forever a part of the rocks and mountain streams.

In the old days, only the staunchest of pilgrims visited the shrines of Gangotri and Jamnotri. The roads were rocky and dangerous, winding along in some places, ascending and descending the faces of deep precipices and ravines, at times leading along banks of loose earth where landslides had swept the original path away. There are still no large towns above Uttarkashi, and this absence of large centres of population may be one reason why the forests are better preserved than, say, those in the Alaknanda valley, or further downstream.

Gangotri is situated at just a little over 10,300 feet and on the right bank of the river is the Gangotri temple. It is a small neat building without too much ornamentation, built by Amar Singh Thapa, a Nepali general, early in the nineteenth century. It was renovated by the Maharaja of Jaipur in the 1920s. The rock on which it stands is called Bhagirath Shila and is said to be the place where Prince Bhagirath did penance in order that Ganga be brought down from her abode of eternal snow.

Here the rocks are carved and polished by ice and water, so smooth that in places they look like rolls of silk. The fast-flowing waters of this mountain torrent look very different from the huge sluggish river that finally empties its waters into the Bay of Bengal 1500 miles away.

The river emerges from beneath a great glacier, thickly studded with enormous loose rocks and earth. The glacier is about a mile in width and extends upwards for many miles. The chasm in the glacier, through which the stream rushes into the light of day, is named Gaumukh, the cow's mouth, and is held in deepest reverence by Hindus. The regions of eternal frost in the vicinity were the scenes of many of their most sacred mysteries.

The Ganga enters the world no puny stream, but bursts from its icy womb a river thirty or forty yards in breadth. At Gauri Kund (below the Gangotri temple) it falls over a rock of considerable height, and continues tumbling over a succession of small cascades until it enters the Bhaironghati gorge.

A night spent beside the river, within sound of the fall, is an eerie experience. After some time it begins to sound, not like one fall but a hundred, and this sound permeates both one's dreams and walking hours. Rising early to greet the dawn proved rather pointless at Gangotri, for the surrounding peaks did not let the sun in till after 9 a.m. Everyone rushes about to keep warm, exclaiming delightedly at what they call *gulabi thand*—literally, 'rosy cold'. Guaranteed to turn the cheeks a rosy pink! A charming expression, but I prefer a rosy sunburn—and remained beneath a heavy quilt until the sun came up to throw its golden shafts across the river.

This is mid-October, and after Diwali the shrine and

the small township will close for the winter, the pandits retreating to the relative warmth of Mukhba. Soon snow will cover everything, and even the hardy purple-plumaged whistling thrushes, lovers of deep shade, will move further down the valley. And down below the forest-line, the Garhwali farmers go about harvesting their ripening paddy, as they have done for centuries; their terraced fields form patterns of yellow, green and gold above the deep green of the river.

Yes, the Bhagirathi is a green river. Although deep and swift, it does not lose its serenity. At no place does it look hurried or confused—unlike the turbulent Alaknanda, fretting and frothing as it goes crashing down its boulder-strewn bed. The Alaknanda gives one a feeling of being trapped, because the river itself is trapped. The Bhagirathi is free-flowing, easy. At all times and places it seems to find its true level.

Uttarkashi, though a large and growing town, is as yet uncrowded. The seediness of over-populated towns like Rishikesh and Dehra Dun is not yet evident here. One can take a leisurely walk through its long (and well-supplied) bazaar, without being jostled by crowds or knocked over by three-wheelers. Here, too, the river is always with you, and you must live in harmony with its sound, as it goes rushing and humming along its shingly bed.

Uttarkashi is not without its own religious and historical importance, although all traces of its ancient capital called Barahat appear to have vanished. There are four important temples here, and on the occasion of Makar Sankranti, early in January, a week-long fair is held, when thousands from the surrounding areas throng the roads to the town. To the beating of drums and blowing of trumpets, the gods and goddesses are brought to the fair in gaily decorated palanquins. The surrounding villages wear a deserted look that day as everyone flocks to the temples and bathing-ghats and to the entertainment of the fair itself.

We have to move far downstream to reach another large centre of population, the town of Tehri, and this is a very different place from Uttarkashi. Tehri has all the characteristics of a small town in the plains—crowds, noise, traffic congestion, dust and refuse, scruffy dhabas— with this difference, that here it is all ephemeral, for Tehri is destined to be submerged by the waters of the Bhagirathi when the Tehri dam is finally completed.

The rulers of Garhwal were often changing their capitals, and when after the Gurkha Wars (1811–15) the former capital of Shrinagar became part of British Garhwal, Raja Sundershan Shah established his new capital at Tehri. It is said that when he reached this spot, his horse refused to go any further. This was enough for the king, it seems; or so the story goes.

Perhaps Prince Bhagirath's chariot will come to a halt here too, when the dam is built. The 246-metre high earthen dam, with forty-two square miles of reservoir capacity, will submerge the town and about thirty villages.

As we leave the town and cross the narrow bridge over the river, a mighty blast from above sends rocks hurtling down the defile, just to remind us that work is in progress.

Unlike the Raja's horse, I have no wish to be stopped in my tracks at Tehri. There are livelier places upstream.

* * *

BEAUTIFUL MANDAKINI

To see a river for the first time at its confluence with another great river is, for me, a special moment in time. And so it was with the Mandakini at Rudraprayag, where its waters were joined with the waters of the Alaknanda, the one having come from the glacial snows above Kedarnath, the other from the Himalayan heights beyond Badrinath. Both sacred rivers, both destined to become the holy Ganga further downstream.

I fell in love with the Mandakini at first sight. Or was it the valley that I fell in love with? I am not sure, and it doesn't really matter. The valley is the river. While the Alaknanda valley, especially in its higher reaches, is a deep and narrow gorge where precipitous outcrops of rock hang threateningly over the traveller, the Mandakini valley is broader, gentler, the terraced fields wider, the banks of the river a green sward in many places.

Rudraprayag is hot. It is probably a pleasant spot in winter, but at the end of June it is decidedly hot. Perhaps its chief claim to fame is that it gave its name to the dreaded man-eating leopard, who, in the course of seven years (1918–25), accounted for more than 300 victims. It was finally shot by the fifty-one-year-old Jim Corbett, who recounted the saga of his long hunt for the killer in his fine book, *The Man-eating Leopard of Rudraprayag*.

The place at which the leopard was shot was the village of Gulabrai, two miles south of Rudraprayag. Under a large mango tree stands a memorial raised to Jim Corbett by officers and men of the Border Roads Organisation. It is a happy gesture to one who loved Garhwal and India. Unfortunately several buffaloes are gathered close by, and one has to wade through slush and buffalo-dung to get to the memorial-stone. A board tacked on to the mango tree attracts the attention of motorists who might pass without noticing the memorial, which is off to one side.

The killer leopard was noted for its direct method of attack on humans; and, in spite of being poisoned, trapped in a cave, and shot at innumerable times, it did not lose its contempt for man. Two English sportsmen covering both ends of the old suspension bridge over the Alaknanda fired several times at the man-eater but to little effect.

It was not long before the leopard acquired a reputation among the hill folk for being an evil spirit. A sadhu was suspected of turning into the leopard by night, and was only saved from being lynched by the ingenuity of Philip Mason, then deputy commissioner of Garhwal. Mason kept the sadhu in custody until the leopard made his next attack, thus proving the man innocent. Years later, when Mason turned novelist and (using the pen-name Philip Woodruff) wrote *The Wild Sweet Witch*, he had as his main character a beautiful young woman who turns into a man-eating leopard by night.

Corbett's host at Gulabrai was one of the few who survived an encounter with the leopard. It left him with a hole in his throat.

Apart from being a superb storyteller, Corbett

displayed great compassion for people from all walks of life and is still a legend in Garhwal and Kumaon amongst people who have never read his books.

In June, one does not linger long in the steamy heat of Rudraprayag. But as one travels up the river, making a gradual ascent of the Mandakini valley, there is a cool breeze coming down from the snows, and the smell of rain is in the air.

The thriving little township of Agastmuni spreads itself along the wide riverbanks, and further upstream, near a little place called Chanderpuri, we cannot resist breaking our journey to sprawl on the tender green grass that slopes gently down to the swiftly flowing river. A small rest-house is in the making. Around it, banana fronds sway and poplar leaves dance in the breeze.

This is no sluggish river of the plains, but a fast moving current, tumbling over rocks, turning and twisting in its efforts to discover the easiest way for its frothy snow-fed waters to escape the mountains. Escape is the word! For the constant plaint of many a Garhwali is that, while his hills abound in rivers the water runs down and away, and little if any reaches the fields and villages above it. Cultivation must depend on the rain and not on the river.

The road climbs gradually, still keeping to the river. Just outside Guptkashi my attention is drawn to a clump of huge trees sheltering a small but ancient temple. We stop here and enter the shade of the trees.

The temple is deserted. It is a temple dedicated to Shiva, and in the courtyard are several river-rounded stone lingams on which leaves and blossoms have fallen. No one seems to come here, which is strange, since it is on the pilgrim route. Two boys from a neighbouring field leave their yoked bullocks to come and talk to me, but they cannot tell me much about the temple except to confirm that it is seldom visited. 'The buses do not stop here.' That seems explanation enough. For where the buses go, the pilgrims go, and where the pilgrims go, other pilgrims will follow. Thus far and no further.

The trees seem to be magnolias, judging by the scent and shape of the flowers, and the boys call them *champa*, Hindi for magnolia blossom. But I have never seen magnolia trees grow to such huge proportions. Perhaps they are something else. Never mind; let them remain a sweet-scented mystery.

Guptkashi in the evening is all a-bustle. A coach-load of pilgrims (headed for Kedarnath) has just arrived, and the tea shops near the bus-stand are doing brisk business. Then the 'local' bus—from Okhimath, across the river—arrives, and many of the passengers head for a tea shop famed for its samosas. The local bus is called the *bhook-hartal*—'hunger-strike'—bus.

'How did it get that name?' I ask one of the samosa-eaters.

'Well, it's an interesting story. For a long time we had been asking the authorities to provide a bus service for the local people and for the villagers who live off the roads. All the buses came from Srinagar or Rishikesh, and were taken up by pilgrims. The locals couldn't find room in them. But our pleas went unheard until the whole town—or most of it, anyway—decided to go on hunger-strike. That worked. And so the bus is named after our successful hunger-strike.'

'They nearly put me out of business too,' said the tea-shop owner cheerfully. 'Nobody ate any samosas for two days!'

There is no cinema or public place of entertainment at Guptkashi, and the town goes to sleep early. And wakes early.

At six, the hillside, green from recent rain, sparkles in the morning sunshine. Snow-capped Chaukhamba (23,400 feet) is dazzling. The air is clear, no smoke or dust up here. The climate, I am told, is mild all the year round. Okhimath, on the other side of the river, lies in the shadow. It gets the sun at 9 a.m. In winter it must wait till afternoon. And yet it seems a bigger place, and by tradition the temple priest from Kedarnath passes winter there when the snows cover that distant shrine.

Guptkashi has not yet been rendered ugly by the barrack-type architecture that has come up in some growing hill towns. The old double-storeyed houses are built of stone, with grey slate roofs. They blend well with the hillside. Cobbled paths meander through the old bazaar.

One of these takes us to the famed Guptkashi temple, tucked away above the old part of the town. Here, as in Benares, Shiva is worshipped as Vishwanath, and two underground streams representing the sacred Yamuna and Bhagirathi rivers feed the pool sacred to the god. This temple gives the town its name—Guptkashi, the 'Invisible Benares', just as Uttarkashi on the Bhagirathi is 'Upper Benares'.

Guptkashi and its environs have so many lingams that the saying *jitne kankar itne Sankar*—'As many stones, so many Shivas'—has become a proverb to describe its holiness.

From Guptkashi, pilgrims proceed north to Kedarnath, and the last stage of their journey—about a day's march—must be covered on foot or horseback. The temple of Kedarnath, situated at a height of 11,753 feet, is encircled by snow-capped peaks, and Atkinson has conjectured that 'the symbol of the linga may have arisen from the pointed peaks around his (God Shiva's) original home'.

The temple is dedicated to Sadashiva, the subterranean form of the god, who, 'fleeing from the Pandavas took refuge here in the form of a he-buffalo'.

We leave the Mandakini to visit Tungnath on the Chandrashila range. But I will return to this river. It has captured my mind and heart.

ON THE ROAD TO BADRINATH

If you travel up the Mandakini valley, and then cross over into the valley of the Alaknanda, you are immediately struck by the contrast. The Mandakini is gentler, richer in vegetation, almost pastoral in places; the Alaknanda is awesome, precipitous, threatening— and seemingly inhospitable to those who must live, and earn a livelihood, in its confines.

Even as we left Chamoli and began the steady, winding climb to Badrinath, the nature of the terrain underwent a dramatic change. No longer did green fields slope gently down to the riverbed. Here they clung precariously to rocky slopes and ledges that grew steeper and narrower, while the river below, impatient to reach its confluence with the Bhagirathi at Deoprayag, thundered along the narrow gorge.

Badrinath is one of the four dhams, or four most

holy places in India. (The other three are Rameshwaram, Dwarka and Jagannath Puri.) For the pilgrim travelling to this holiest of holies, the journey is exciting, possibly even uplifting; but for those who live permanently on these crags and ridges, life is harsh, a struggle from one day to the next. No wonder so many young men from Garhwal find their way into the Army. Little grows on these rocky promontories; and what does, is at the mercy of the weather. For most of the year the fields lie fallow. Rivers, unfortunately, run downhill and not uphill.

The harshness of this life, typical of much of Garhwal, was brought home to me at Pipalkoti, where we stopped for the night. Pilgrims stop here by the coachload, for the Garhwal Mandal Vikas Nigam's rest-house is fairly capacious, and small hotels and dharamshalas abound. Just off the busy road is a tiny hospital, and here, late in the evening, we came across a woman keeping vigil over the dead body of her husband. The body had been laid out on a bench in the courtyard. A few feet away the road was crowded with pilgrims in festival mood; no one glanced over the low wall to notice this tragic scene.

The woman came from a village near Helong. Earlier that day, finding her consumptive husband in a critical condition she had decided to bring him to the nearest town for treatment. As he was frail and emaciated, she was able to carry him on her back for several miles, until she reached the motor road. Then, at some expense, she engaged a passing taxi and brought him to Pipalkoti. But he was already dead when she reached the small hospital. There was no morgue; so she sat beside the body in the courtyard, waiting for dawn and the arrival of others from the village. A few men arrived next morning and we saw them winding their way down to the cremation ground. We did not see the woman again. Her children were hungry and she had to hurry home to look after them.

Pipalkoti is hot (and peepul trees are conspicuous by their absence), but Joshimath, the winter resort of the Badrinath temple establishment, is about 6000 feet above sea level and has an equable climate. It is now a fairly large town, and although the surrounding hills are rather bare, it does have one great tree that has survived the ravages of time. This is an ancient mulberry, known as the Kalpa Vriksha (Immortal Wishing Tree), beneath which the great Sankaracharya meditated a few centuries ago. It is reputedly over two thousand years old, and is certainly larger than my modest four-roomed flat in Mussoorie. Sixty pilgrims holding hands might just about encircle its trunk.

I have seen some big trees, but this is certainly the

oldest and broadest of them. I am glad the Sankaracharya meditated beneath it and thus ensured its preservation. Otherwise it might well have gone the way of other great trees and forests that once flourished in this area.

A small boy reminds me that it is a Wishing Tree, so I make my wish. I wish that other trees might prosper like this one.

'Have you made a wish?' I ask the boy.

'I wish that you will give me one rupee,' he says.

His wish comes true with immediate effect. Mine lies in the uncertain future. But he has given me a lesson in wishing.

Joshimath has to be a fairly large place, because most of Badrinath arrives here in November, when the shrine is snowbound for six months. Army and PWD structures also dot the landscape. This is no carefree hill resort, but it has all the amenities for making a short stay quite pleasant and interesting. Perched on the steep mountainside above the junction of the Alaknanda and Dhauli rivers, it is now vastly different from what it was when Frank Smythe visited it fifty years ago and described it as 'an ugly little place . . . straggling unbeautifully over the hillside. Primitive little shops line the main street, which is roughly paved in places and in others has been deeply channelled by the monsoon rains. The pilgrims spend the night in single-storeyed rest-houses, not unlike the hovels provided for the kentish hop-pickers of former days, some of which are situated in narrow passages running off the main street and are filthy and evil-smelling.'

Those were Joshimath's former days. It is a different place today, with small hotels, modern shops, a cinema; and its growth and comparative modernity date from the early 1960s, when the old pilgrim footpath gave way to the motor road which takes the traveller all the way to Badrinath. No longer does the weary, footsore pilgrim sink gratefully down in the shade of the Kalpa Vriksha. He alights from his bus or luxury coach and drinks a cola at one of the many small restaurants on the roadside.

Contrast this comfortable journey with the pilgrimage fifty years ago. Frank Smythe again:

So they venture on their pilgrimage . . . Some borne magnificently by coolies, some toiling along in rags, some almost crawling, preyed on by disease and distorted by dreadful deformities . . . Europeans who have read and travelled cannot conceive what goes on in the minds of these simple folk, many of them from the

agricultural parts of India, wonderment and fear
must be the prime ingredients. So the pilgrimage
becomes an adventure. Unknown dangers
threaten the broad well-made path, at any
moment the gods, who hold the rocks in leash,
may unloose their wrath upon the hapless
passers-by. To the European it is a walk to
Badrinath, to the Hindu pilgrim it is far, far
more.

Above Vishnuprayag, Smythe left the Alaknanda and
entered the Bhyundar valley, a botanist's paradise, which
he called the Valley of Flowers. He fell in love with the
lush meadows of this high valley, and made it known to
the world. It continues to attract the botanist and trekker.
Primulas of subtle shades, wild geraniums, saxifrages
clinging to the rocks, yellow and red potentillas, snow-
white anemones, delphiniums, violets, wild roses, all
these and many more flourish there, capturing the mind
and heart of the flower-lover.

'Impossible to take a step without crushing a flower.'
This may not be true any more, for many footsteps have
trodden the Bhyundar in recent years. There are other
areas in Garhwal where the hills are rich in flora—the
Har-ki-doon, Harsil, Tungnath, and the Khiraun valley

where the balsam grows to a height of eight feet—but the Bhyunder has both a variety and a concentration of wild flowers, especially towards the end of the monsoon. It would be no exaggeration to call it one of the most beautiful valleys in the world.

The Bhyundar is a digression for lovers of mountain scenery; but the pilgrim keeps his eyes fixed on the ultimate goal—Badrinath, where 'the gods dwelt and where salvation is to be found'.

There are still a few who do it the hard way—mostly those who have taken sanyas and renounced the world. Here is one hardy soul doing penance. He stretches himself out on the ground, draws himself up to a standing position, then flattens himself out again. In this manner he will proceed from Badrinath to Rishikesh, oblivious of the sun and rain, the dust from passing buses, the sharp gravel of the footpath.

Others are not so hardy. One saffron-robed scholar, speaking fair English, asks us for a lift to Badrinath, and we find space for him. He rewards us with a long and involved commentary on the Vedas, which lasts through the remainder of the journey. His special field of study, he informs us, is the part played by Aeronautics in Vedic literature.

'And what,' I ask him, 'is the connection between the two?'

He looks at me pityingly.

'It is what I am trying to find out,' he replies.

The road drops to Pandukeshwar and rises again, and all the time I am scanning the horizon for the forests of the Badrinath region I had read about many years ago in Fraser's Himalaya Mountains! Walnuts growing up to 9000 feet, deodars and 'Bilka' up to 9500 feet, and 'Amesh' and 'Kiusu' fir at a similar height—but, apart from strands of long leaved excelsia pine, I do not see much, certainly no deodars. What has happened to them, I wonder. An endless variety of trees delighted us all the way from Dugalbeta to Mandal, a well-protected area, but here on the high ridges above the Alaknanda, little seems to grow; or, if ever they did, have long since been bespoiled or swept away.

Finally we reach the windswept, barren valley which harbours Badrinath—a growing township, thriving, lively, but somewhat dwarfed by the snow-capped peaks that tower above it. As at Joshimath, there is no dearth of hostelries and dharamshalas. Even so, every hotel or rest-house is filled to overflowing. It is the height of the pilgrim season, and pilgrims, tourists and mendicants of every description throng the river-front.

Just as Kedar is the most sacred of the Shiva temples in the Himalayas, so Badrinath is the supreme place of worship for the Vaishnav sects.

According to legend, when Sankaracharya in his digvijaya travels visited the Mana valley he arrived at the Narada-Kund and found fifty different images lying in its waters. These he rescued, and when he had done so, a voice from Heaven said, 'These are the images for the Kaliyug, establish them here.' Sankaracharya accordingly placed them beneath a mighty tree which grew there and whose shade extended from Badrinath to Nandprayag, a distance of over eighty miles. Close to it was the hermitage of Nar-Narayana (or Arjuna and Krishna), and in course of time temples were built in honour of these and other manifestations of Vishnu. It was here that Vishnu appeared to his followers in person, as the four-armed, crested and adorned with pearls and garlands. The faithful, it is said, can still see him on the peak of Nilkantha, on the great Kumbha day. It is, in fact, the Nilkantha peak that dominates this crater-like valley where a few hardy thistles and nettles manage to survive. Like cacti in the desert, the pricklier forms of life seem best equipped to live in a hostile environment.

Nilkantha means blue-necked, an allusion to the god Shiva's swallowing of a poison meant to destroy the world. The poison remained in his throat, which was rendered blue thereafter. It is a majestic and awe-inspiring peak, soaring to a height of 21,640 feet. As its summit is only five miles from Badrinath, it is justly held in reverence. From its ice-clad pinnacle three great ridges sweep down, of which the southern one terminates in the Alaknanda valley.

On the evening of our arrival we could not see the peak, as it was hidden in clouds. Badrinath itself was shrouded in mist. But we made our way to the temple, a gaily decorated building about fifty feet high, with a gilded roof. The image of Vishnu, carved in black stone, stands in the centre of the sanctum, opposite the door, in a Dhyana posture. An endless stream of people passes through the temple to pay homage and emerge the better for their proximity to the divine.

From the temple, flights of steps lead down to the rushing river and to the hot springs which emerge just above it. Another road leads through a long but tidy bazaar where pilgrims may buy mementos of their visit. Here at last I am free to indulge my passion for cheap rings, with none to laugh at my foible. There are all kinds, from rings designed like a coiled serpent (my favourite) to twisted bands of copper and iron and others containing the pictures of gods, gurus and godmen. They do not cost more than two or three rupees each, and so I am able to fill my pockets. I never wear these rings. I simply hoard them away. My friends are convinced that in a previous existence I was a jackdaw, seizing upon and hiding away any kind of bright and shiny object: So be it . . .

Even those who have renounced the world appear to be cheerful—like the young woman from Gujarat who had taken sanyas and who met me on the steps below the temple. She gave me a dazzling smile and passed me an exercise book. She had taken a vow of silence; but being, I think, of an extrovert nature, she seemed eager to remain in close communication with the rest of humanity, and did so by means of written questions and answers. Hence the exercise book.

Although, at Badrinath, I missed the sound of birds and the presence of trees, it was good to be part of the happy throng at its colourful little temple, and to see the sacred river close to its source. And early next morning I was rewarded with the liveliest experience of all.

Opening the window of my room, and glancing out, I saw the rising sun touch the snow-clad summit of Nilkantha. At first the snows were pink; then they turned to orange and gold. All sleep vanished as I gazed up in wonder at that magnificent pinnacle in the sky. And had Lord Vishnu appeared just then on the summit, I would not have been in the least surprised.

THE MAGIC OF TUNGNATH

The mountains and valleys of Garhwal never fail to spring surprises on the traveller in search of the picturesque. It is impossible to know every corner of the Himalayas, which means that there are always new corners to discover; forest or meadow, mountain stream or wayside shrine.

The temple of Tungnath, at a little over 12,000 feet, is the highest shrine on the inner Himalayan range. It lies just below the Chandrashila peak. Some way off the main pilgrim routes, it is less frequented than Kedamath or Badrinath, although it forms a part of the Kedar temple establishment. The priest here is a local man, a Brahmin from the village of Maku; the other Kedar temples have South Indian priests, a tradition begun by Sankaracharya, the eighth-century Hindu reformer and revivalist.

Tungnath's lonely eminence gives it a magic of its own. To get there (or beyond it), one passes through some of the most delightful temperate forest in the Garhwal Himalayas. Pilgrim or trekker, or just plain rambler like myself, one comes away a better man, forest-refreshed and more aware of what the world was really like before mankind began to strip it bare.

Duiri Tal, a small lake, lies cradled on the hill above Okhimath at a height of 8000 feet. It was a favourite spot of one of Garhwal's earliest British commissioners, J.H. Batten, whose administration continued for twenty years (1836–56). He wrote:

> The day I reached there it was snowing and young trees were laid prostrate under the weight of snow, the lake was frozen over to a depth of about two inches. There was no human habitation and the place looked a veritable wilderness. The next morning when the sun appeared, the Chaukhamba and many other peaks extending as far as Kedarnath seemed covered with a new quilt of snow as if close at hand. The whole scene was so exquisite that one could not tire of gazing at it for hours. I think a person who has a subdued settled despair in his mind would all

of a sudden feel a kind of bounding and exalting
cheerfulness which will be imparted to his frame
by the atmosphere of Duiri Tal.

This feeling of uplift can be experienced almost anywhere
along the Tungnath range. Duiri Tal is still some way off
the beaten track and anyone wishing to spend the night
there should carry a tent. But further along this range,
the road ascends to Dugalbeta (at about 9000 feet) where
a PWD rest-house, gaily painted, has come up like some
exotic orchid in the midst of a lush meadow topped by
excelsia pines and pencil cedars. Many an official who
has stayed here has rhapsodized on the charms of
Dugalbeta; and if you are unofficial (and therefore not
entitled to stay in the bungalow), you can move on to
Chopta, lusher still, where there is accommodation of a
sort for pilgrims and other hardy souls. Two or three
little tea shops provide mattresses and quilts. The Garhwal
Mandal has a rest-house there. These tourist rest-houses
scattered over the length and breadth of Garhwal, are a
great boon to the traveller; but during the pilgrim season
(May–June) they are filled to overflowing and if you turn
up unexpectedly you might have to take your pick of tea
shop or dharamshala, a lucky dip, since they vary a good
deal in comfort and cleanliness.

The trek from Chopta to Tungnath is only three and a half miles, but in that distance one ascends about 3000 feet, and the pilgrim may be forgiven for feeling that at places he is on a perpendicular path. 'Like a ladder to heaven,' I couldn't help thinking.

In spite of its steepness, my companion, the redoubtable Ganesh Saili, insisted that we take a short cut. After clawing our way up tufts of alpine grass which formed the rungs of our ladder, we were stuck and had to inch our way down again so that the ascent of Tungnath began to resemble a game of Snakes and Ladders.

A tiny guardian temple dedicated to the god Ganesh spurred us on. Nor was I really fatigued for the cold fresh air and the verdant greenery surrounding us was like an intoxicant. Myriads of wild flowers grew on the hill slopes—buttercups, anemones, wild strawberries, forget-me-nots, rock-cress—enough to rival the Valley of Flowers at this time of the year.

Before reaching these alpine meadows, we climb through rhododendron forest and here one finds at least three species of this flower: the red flowering-tree rhododendron (found throughout the Himalayas between 6000 feet and 10,000 feet); a second variety, the almatta, with flowers that are light red or rosy in colour; and the third, chimul, or white variety, found at heights ranging from between 10,000 feet and 13,000 feet. The chimul is brushwood, seldom more than twelve feet high and growing slantingly due to the heavy burden of snow it has to carry for almost six months in the year.

Those brushwood rhododendrons are the last trees we see on our ascent for as we approach Tungnath the treeline ends and there is nothing between earth and sky except grass and rock and tiny flowers. Above us, a couple of crows dive-bomb a hawk, who does his best to escape their attentions. Crows are the world's great survivors. They are capable of living at any height and in any climate; as much at home in the back streets of Delhi as on the heights of Tungnath.

Another survivor, up here at any rate, is the pika, a sort of mouse-hare, who looks like neither mouse nor hare but rather a tiny guinea-pig; small ears, no tail, grey-brown fur and chubby feet. They emerge from their holes under the rocks to forage for grasses on which to feed. Their simple diet and thick fur enable them to live in extreme cold and they have been found at 16,000 feet; no other mammal is known to live at a greater height. The Garhwalis call this little creature the runda—at any rate, that's what the temple priest called it, adding that it was not averse to entering his house and helping itself to grain and other delicacies. So perhaps there's more in it of mouse than of hare.

Those little rundas were with us all the way from Chopta to Tungnath, peering out from their rocks and scampering about on the hillside, seemingly unconcerned by our presence.

At Tungnath they live beneath the temple flagstones. The priest's grandchildren were having a game discovering their burrows; the rundas would go in at one hole and pop out at another—they must have had a system of underground passages.

When we arrived, clouds had gathered over Tungnath, as they do almost every afternoon. The temple looked austere in the gathering gloom.

To some, the name 'Tung' indicates 'lofty', from the position of the temple on the highest peak outside the main chain of the Himalayas; others derive it from the word *tangna*—to be suspended—in allusion to the form under which the deity is worshipped here. The form is the Swayambhu Ling; and on Shivaratri, or night of Shiva, the true believer may, 'with the eye of faith', see the lingam increase in size; but 'to the evil-minded no such favour is granted'.

The temple, though not very large, is certainly impressive, mainly because of its setting and the solid

slabs of grey granite from which it is built. The whole
place somehow puts me in mind of Emily Brontë's
Wuthering Heights—bleak, windswept, open to the skies.
And as you look down from the temple at the little half-
deserted hamlet that serves it in summer, the eye is met
by grey slate roofs and piles of stones, with just a few
hardy souls in residence—for the majority of pilgrims
now prefer to spend the night down at Chopta.

Even the temple priest, attended by his son and
grandsons, complains bitterly of the cold. To spend every
day barefoot on those flagstones must indeed be hardship.
I wince after five minutes of it, made worse by stepping
into a puddle of icy water. I shall never make a good
pilgrim; no rewards for me, in this world or the next. But
the priest's feet are literally thick-skinned; and the
children seem oblivious to the cold. Still, in October they
must be happy to descend to Maku, their home village
on the slopes below Dugalbeta.

It begins to rain as we leave the temple. We pass
herds of sheep huddled in a ruined dharamshala. The
crows are still rushing about the grey weeping skies,
although the hawk has very sensibly gone away. A
runda sticks his nose out from his hole, probably to take
a look at the weather. There is a clap of thunder and he

disappears, like the White Rabbit in 'Alice in Wonderland'. We are halfway down the Tungnath 'ladder' when it begins to rain quite heavily. And now we pass our first genuine pilgrims, a group of intrepid Bengalis who are heading straight into the storm. They are without umbrellas or raincoats, but they are not to be deterred.

Oaks and rhododendrons flash past as we dash down the steep, winding path. Another shortc ut and Ganesh Saili takes a tumble, but is cushioned by moss and buttercups. My wristwatch strikes a rock and the glass is shattered. No matter. Time here is of little or no significance. Away with time! Is this, I wonder, the 'bounding and exalting cheerfulness' experienced by Batten and now manifesting in me?

The tea shop beckons. How would one manage in the hills without these wayside tea shops? Miniature inns, they provide food, shelter and even lodging to dozens at a time.

We sit on a bench between a Gujjar herdsman and a pilgrim who is too feverish to make the climb to the temple. He accepts my offer of an aspirin to go with his tea. We tackle some buns—rock-hard, to match our environment—and wash the pellets with hot sweet tea.

There is a small shrine here, too, right in front of the

tea shop. It is a slab of rock roughly shaped like a lingam and it is daubed with vermilion and strewn with offerings of wild flowers. The mica in the rock gives it a beautiful sheen.

I suppose Hinduism comes closest to being a nature religion. Rivers, rocks, trees, plants, animals and birds all play their part, both in mythology and in everyday worship. This harmony is most evident in those remote places where gods and mountains coexist. Tungnath, as yet unspoilt by materialistic society, exerts its magic on all who come there with open mind and heart.

THE GLACIER

It was a fine sunny morning—oh so many years ago—when we set out to cover the last seven miles to the glacier, Kamal, Anil, Bisnu and I. We were young, hungry for adventure. We had expected this to be a stiff climb, and it was. The last dak bungalow was situated at well over 10,000 feet above sea level, and the ascent was to be fairly gradual.

And suddenly, abruptly, there were no more trees. As the bungalow dropped out of sight, the trees and bushes gave way to short grass and little blue-and-pink alpine flowers. The snow-peaks were close now, ringing us in on every side. We passed waterfalls, cascading hundreds of feet down precipitous rock faces, thundering into the little river. A great golden eagle hovered over us for some time.

'I feel different again,' said Kamal.

'We're very high now,' I said. 'I hope we won't get headaches.'

'I've got one already,' complained Anil. 'Let's have some tea.'

We had left our cooking utensils at the bungalow, expecting to return there for the night, and had brought with us only a few biscuits, chocolate and a thermos of tea. We finished the tea, and Bisnu scrambled about on the grassy slopes, collecting wild strawberries. They were tiny strawberries, very sweet, and they did nothing to satisfy our appetites. There was no sign of habitation or human life. The only creatures to be found at that height were the gurals—sure-footed mountain goats—and an occasional snow-leopard, or a bear.

We found and explored a small cave, and then turning a bend, came unexpectedly upon the glacier.

The hill fell away and there, confronting us, was a great white field of snow and ice cradled between two peaks that could only have been the abode of the gods. We were speechless for several minutes. Kamal took my hand and held on to it for reassurance; perhaps he was not sure that what he saw was real. Anil's mouth hung open. Bisnu's eyes glittered with excitement.

We proceeded cautiously on to the snow, supporting each other on the slippery surface, but we could not go

far, because we were quite unequipped for any high-altitude climbing. It was pleasant to feel that we were the only boys in our town who had climbed so high. A few black rocks jutted out from the snow, and we sat down on them, to feast our eyes on the view. The sun reflected sharply from the snow, and we felt surprisingly warm.

'Let's sunbathe!' said Anil, on a sudden impulse.

'Yes, let's do that!' I said.

In a few minutes we had taken off our clothes and, sitting on the rocks, were exposing ourselves to the elements. It was delicious to feel the sun crawling over my skin. Within half an hour I was postbox red, and so was Bisnu, and the two of us decided to get into our clothes before the sun scorched the skin off our backs. Kamal and Anil appeared to be more resilient to sunlight, and laughed at our discomfiture. Bisnu and I avenged ourselves by gathering up handfuls of snow and rubbing it on their backs. They dressed quickly enough after that, Anil leaping about like a performing monkey.

Meanwhile, almost imperceptibly, clouds had covered some of the peaks, and a white mist drifted down the mountain slopes. It was time to get back to the bungalow; we would barely make it before dark.

We had not gone far when lightning began to sizzle above the mountain-tops, followed by waves of thunder.

'Let's run!' shouted Anil. 'We can take shelter in the cave!'

The clouds could hold themselves in no longer, and the rain came down suddenly, stinging our faces as it was whipped up by an icy wind. Half-blinded, we ran as fast as we could along the slippery path, and stumbled, drenched and exhausted, into the little cave.

The cave was mercifully dry, and not very dark. We remained at the entrance, watching the rain sweep past us, listening to the wind whistling down the long gorge.

'It will take some time to stop,' said Kamal.

'No, it will pass soon,' said Bisnu. 'These storms are short and fierce.'

Anil produced his pocket knife, and to pass the time we carved our names in the smooth rock of the cave.

'We will come here again, when we are older,' said Kamal, 'and perhaps our names will still be here.'

It had grown dark by the time the rain stopped. A full moon helped us find our way. We went slowly and carefully. The rain had loosened the earth and stones kept rolling down the hillside. I was afraid of sporting a landslide.

'I hope we don't meet the Lidini now,' said Anil fervently.

'I thought you didn't believe in her,' I said.

'I don't,' replied Anil. 'But what if I'm wrong?'

We saw only a gural, poised on the brow of a precipice, silhouetted against the sky.

And then the path vanished.

Had it not been for the bright moonlight, we might have walked straight into an empty void. The rain had caused a landslide, and where there had been a narrow path there was now only a precipice of loose, slippery shale.

'We'll have to go back,' said Bisnu. 'It will be too

dangerous to try and cross in the dark.'

'We'll sleep in the cave,' I suggested.

'We've nothing to sleep in,' said Anil. 'Not a single blanket between us—and nothing to eat!'

'We'll just have to rough it till morning,' said Kamal. 'It will be better than breaking our necks here.'

We returned to the cave, which did at least have the virtue of being dry. Bisnu had matches, and he made a fire with some dry sticks which had been left in the cave by a previous party. We ate what was left of a loaf of bread.

There was no sleep for any of us that night. We lay close to each other for comfort, but the ground was hard and uneven. And every noise we heard outside the cave made us think of leopards and bears and even the Abominable Snowman.

We got up as soon as there was a faint glow in the sky. The snow peaks were bright pink, but we were too tired and hungry and worried to care for the beauty of the sunrise. We took the path to the landslide, and once again looked for a way across. Kamal ventured to take a few steps on the loose pebbles, but the ground gave way immediately, and we had to grab him by the arms and shoulders to prevent him from sliding a hundred feet down the gorge.

'Now what are we going to do?' I asked.

'Look for another way,' said Bisnu.

'But do you know of any?'

And we all turned to look at Bisnu, expecting him to provide the solution to our problem.

'I have heard of a way,' said Bisnu. 'But I have never used it. It will be a little dangerous, I think. The path has not been used for several years—not since the traders stopped coming in from Tibet.'

'Never mind, we'll try it,' said Anil.

'We will have to cross the glacier first,' said Bisnu. 'That's the main problem.'

We looked at each other in silence. The glacier didn't look difficult to cross, but we knew that it would not be easy for novices. For almost two furlongs it consisted of hard, slippery ice.

Anil was the first to arrive at a decision.

'Come on,' he said. 'There's no time to waste.'

We were soon on the glacier. And we remained on it for a long time. For every two steps forward, we slid one step backward. Our progress was slow and awkward. Sometimes, after advancing several yards across the ice at a steep incline, one of us would slip back and the others would have to slither down to help him up. At one particularly difficult spot, I dropped our water bottle and grabbing at it, lost my footing, fell full-length and went sliding some twenty feet down the ice slope.

I had sprained my wrist and hurt my knee and was to prove a liability for the rest of the trek.

Kamal tied his handkerchief round my hand, and Anil took charge of the water bottle, which we had filled with ice. Using my good hand to grab Bisnu's legs whenever I slipped, I struggled on behind the others.

It was almost noon and we were quite famished by the time we put our feet on grass again. And then we had another steep climb, clutching at roots and grasses, before we reached the path that Bisnu had spoken about. It was little more than a goat-track, but it took us round the mountain and brought us within sight of the dak bungalow.

'I could eat a whole chicken,' said Kamal.

'I could eat two,' I said.

'I could eat a snowman,' said Bisnu.

'And I could eat the chowkidar,' said Anil.

Fortunately for the chowkidar, he had anticipated our hunger, and when we staggered into the bungalow late in the afternoon, we found a meal waiting for us. True, there was no chicken—but, so ravenous did we feel, that even the lowly onion tasted delicious!

We had Bisnu to thank for getting us back

successfully. He had brought us over mountain and glacier with all the skill and confidence of a boy who had the Himalayas in his blood.

We took our time getting back to Kapkote. We fished in the Sarayu river, bathed with the village boys we had seen on our way up, collected strawberries and ferns and wild flowers, and finally said goodbye to Bisnu.

Anil wanted to take Bisnu along with us, but the boy's parents refused to let him go, saying that he was too young for the life in a city; but we were of the opinion that Bisnu could have taught the city boys a few things.

'Never mind,' said Kamal. 'We'll go on another trip next year, and we'll take you with us, Bisnu. We'll write and let you know our plans.'

This promise made Bisnu happy, and he saw us off at the bus stop, shouldering our bedding to the end. Then he skimmed up the trunk of a fir tree to have a better view of us leaving, and we saw him waving to us from the tree as our bus went round the bend from Kapkote, and the hills were left behind and the plains stretched out below.